# Secure Operations Technology

# Secure Operations Technology

**Andrew Ginter**
**www.sec-ot.ca**

Abterra Technologies Inc.
Calgary

## WARNING

## EXAMPLES

While the industrial control system design examples and case studies in this book are inspired by the author's experience with real sites, all are hypothetical - none literally or accurately describe any real site in this author's experience.

Published by Abterra Technologies Inc.
Calgary, Alberta, Canada
www.abterra.ca


ISBN 978-0-9952984-2-2 (softcover)
ISBN 978-0-9952984-3-9 (hardcover)
First printing.

*To Betty, with love*

Secure Operations Technology

# Contents

# Foreword

As 2018 comes to a close, one thing I predict we can count on is the continued expansion of the threat landscape for Industrial Control Systems (ICS) – commonly referred to as Operational Technology (OT).

Our nations, our way of life, and perhaps our very survival depend on critical infrastructures such as water, energy and food supply. All these industries have become automated and are heavily reliant on computerized systems such as ICS, SCADA and OT. These and all systems that are cyber in nature, but especially those with bidirectional network connections of any kind, are vulnerable to cyber attack.

I have worked with Andrew Ginter for over a decade, as we waged awareness campaigns in industrial cybersecurity, and cooperated in other initiatives, often through public-private partnerships such as the U.S. Department of Homeland Security's (DHS) Industrial Control Systems Joint Working Group (ICSJWG). As the longest serving and last Director of the DHS Industrial Control Systems Cyber Emergency Response Team (ICS-CERT), which is now part of the National Cybersecurity and Communications Integration Center (NCCIC), I know most of the "movers and shakers" in this industry and Andrew has been a key contributor over all these years.

Once realized only through research experiments such as the Aurora Generator Test performed by the Idaho National Laboratory (INL) for DHS in 2007, attacks on the OT infrastructures around us are quite real and can in fact result in dangerous consequences and life-threatening effects:

- Hundreds of thousands of people without electricity during the dead of winter – these outages were the result of Ukraine power grid cyber attacks in 2015 and 2016.

- Operating a dangerous process without the protection of the Safety Instrumented System (SIS) which is designed for one thing only – to keep plant personnel and equipment safe by performing specific shutdown functions when dangerous conditions arise. This was apparently the intended result of the Trisis-Triton-Hatman cyber attack in 2017.

Events such as these and others underscore the importance of Secure Operations Technology. In this book, Andrew describes various scenarios utilizing unidirectional gateway technologies that significantly improve the scenarios' cybersecurity.

Control systems like these are the cornerstone of many industrial and critical infrastructure operations, and as such contain valuable data that must be exposed and made available to the overall business in order to achieve maximum efficiencies and capabilities.

Cybersecurity solutions such as the "air gap" hinder our abilities to capitalize on these valuable data assets. Coincidentally, the "air gap" can also hamper cybersecurity efforts by making initiatives such as real-time intrusion detection impossible to achieve due to the lack of full-time network connectivity.

A holistic and thorough security program has many complex, time-consuming and costly aspects that are essential to what is widely considered due diligence for such critical systems. Areas such as governance and policy, asset inventory, risk assessment, patch management, intrusion detection, incident response and so on are absolutely vital to a well-rounded program and should be addressed in due time.

This book and Andrew's approach take somewhat of a shortcut and give owners and operators of critical infrastructure the opportunity to get the most "bang for the buck" early on in their cybersecurity investment life cycle.

By properly utilizing the "physics-based" one-way communications properties of unidirectional technologies, you can be virtually guaranteed to foil any network intruder. You must certainly consider other intrusion vectors in your cybersecurity program, but network-based attacks are by far the most common infection vector. A one-way connection makes available the valuable real-time information inside the OT system while at the same time thwarting the would-be inbound network attacker.

Attacks on critical infrastructures, ICS and OT will become more frequent, sophisticated and damaging – so it is imperative that owners and operators implement straightforward network segmentation initiatives in concert with properly designed one-way communications strategies to ensure protection of these "most critical" of critical networks.

Our nations, our way of life, and perhaps our very survival depend on critical infrastructures such as water, energy and food supply. Isn't it about time we started to protect them with that in mind?

*Marty Edwards*
*December 2018*

# Acknowledgements

The best practices and insights I relate in this book are drawn from a decade of experience working with Lior Frenkel, CEO and Co-Founder of Waterfall Security Solutions, Tomer Maor, VP Customer Service and Operations, and other Waterfall Security Solutions employees and customers, as well as a wide variety of other security experts. My heartfelt thanks to all these people who contributed to my understanding of the practices and principles I document here.

I also thank my dedicated reviewers for their very valuable feedback: Dr. Arthur Conklin, Dr. Jesus Molina, Andrea Ginter, Caroline Tabach, Mike Firstenberg, Courtney Schneider, Alan Dewar, Rachel Ginter, Betty Wong, and Lior Frenkel.

For the record, while I am grateful to everyone who has contributed to this book and to my understanding of these issues, no reader should assume that any of these good people agree with anything I have written. In fact, most of them have expressed disagreement with at least some of the points I make. This book expresses my own opinions, not necessarily those of anyone else.

*Andrew Ginter*

# Chapter 1  Introduction

This book describes the Secure Operations Technology (SEC-OT) perspective, methodology and set of best practices for securing industrial control systems (ICS) from cyber threats. This chapter introduces SEC-OT and very broadly outlines how SEC-OT differs from Information Technology Security (IT-SEC).

SEC-OT is focused on cyber security for physical operations. To this end, SEC-OT defines control system security as:

---

**Definition**

**Control system security** – *protecting the safe and reliable control of physical operations from attacks embedded in information*

---

Important elements in this definition include:

*Safety:* The first priority at all SEC-OT sites is safety. Safety is defined as preventing unacceptable risks of casualties at the site, threats to the public in nearby communities, and environmental disasters.

*Reliability:* The second priority at SEC-OT sites is reliable operation of the physical process. Reliable operation includes correct, efficient and continuous physical operations. Unscheduled downtime, production quality failures and equipment damage are all examples of reliability failures.

*Control:* Industrial operations at SEC-OT sites are computer-controlled. Correct and authorized control of the computers that in turn control the physical process are essential to safe and reliable operations.

*Information:* All attacks are information – the goal of SEC-OT is not to protect the information but to protect physical operations from attacks embedded in information. The key difference between SEC-OT and IT-SEC is therefore:

---

**Note**

**IT-SEC** – *protect the information*

**SEC-OT** – *protect physical operations from information, or more specifically, from attacks that may be embedded in information*

---

This difference in perspective has profound implications. For example:

- The classic "encrypt everything" IT-SEC response to protecting information has limited value in SEC-OT – all cyber attacks are information, and attack information can be encrypted just as easily as legitimate information.

- IT-SEC consequences of compromise are business consequences, such as damaged reputations, lawsuits and computers that need to be erased and restored from backups. SEC-OT consequences are physical consequences and generally cannot be "restored from backups."

- The IT-SEC philosophy of "let information flow where it will, so long as the information is protected" is directly at odds with the SEC-OT philosophy of controlling the flow of attacks by thoroughly limiting and controlling the flow of information.

Once physical operations are protected from cyber compromise though, preventing the theft of certain kinds of information is also important at many industrial sites. Production formulas, recipes and other intellectual property, for example, may need protection from unauthorized disclosure. SEC-OT designs and best practices are always augmented with IT-SEC technologies and approaches, both to protect trade secrets and as a second line of software-based defences for safe and reliable operations.

## SEC-OT Principles

The first three SEC-OT principles mirror the first three laws of control system security coined in this author's book *SCADA Security – What's broken and how to fix it.* The three laws are paraphrased:

---

### *First Three Laws of Control System Security*

1. *Nothing is secure – security is a continuum, not a binary value.*

2. *All software can be hacked – all software has defects, and some defects are exploitable vulnerabilities.*

3. *All cyber attacks are information, and every piece of information can be an attack.*

---

The corresponding SEC-OT design principles are:

---

**SEC-OT Principles**

1. *To understand cyber risk, understand which attacks and consequences a security program does not defeat reliably.*

2. *To survive software compromise, physically protect control-critical networks from cyber attacks.*

3. *To control attacks, inventory and control information flows.*

---

## Understanding Attacks

No security posture is perfect – given enough time, talent and money, any security posture can be breached. This means that every industrial control system, no matter how thoroughly protected, has residual risks due to cyber attacks. Businesses generally either:

- Mitigate these risks by changing the design of control systems or security programs to eliminate the risks,

- Transfer the risks for a fee to a willing insurer, or

- Accept the risks and if an attack occurs, suffer the consequences.

Understanding residual risks is therefore very important to business decision-making. Decision makers should understand the risks they accept on behalf of the business rather than accept risks blindly. Chapters 10-12 provide an example of a SEC-OT-compatible, capabilities-based approach to risk assessment using a standard set of 20 ICS cyber attacks.

## Physical Protection

All software can be compromised by cyber attacks, including security software, cryptosystems and firewalls. Almost all software can be misconfigured as well, and modern attackers generally find it easier to exploit permissions than to exploit software vulnerabilities. For these reasons, SEC-OT requires physical rather than software-based protections.

For example, a security design that puts control-critical and IT computers both on the same physical switch and separates the two using VLAN software violates the physical-protection principle. If an attacker steals the password for the VLAN system, it is a simple matter to disable the VLAN and so eliminate the software separation between networks.

> **Note**
>
> *SEC-OT does not demand physical protection for all information flows, only for flows into control-critical networks from external networks, such as IT networks or the Internet that are not managed according to SEC-OT principles.*

Chapters 4-6 explore physical protections from both offline and online attacks.

## Controlling Information and Attack Flows

All cyber attacks are information, and all information can encode attacks, therefore any comprehensive list of information flows into a control system is also a comprehensive list of attack vectors. The only way that a control system can change from an uncompromised to a compromised state is for attack information to cross a physical or network perimeter into the control system from outside the system.

> **Note**
>
> *This book routinely uses the term "information/attack flow" instead of "information flow" or "attack flow" to highlight the fact that all attacks are information, and every piece of information can encode an attack.*

Because any information can contain an attack, the SEC-OT ideal is the elimination of all information/attack flows from noncritical networks into control-critical networks. This ideal is generally impossible to achieve. SEC-OT principles and best practices dramatically reduce information/ attack flows from noncritical networks but generally cannot eliminate all such flows. SEC-OT, therefore, also demands strong procedures and technologies for inspecting, testing and validating residual offline and online information/attack flows.

> **Note**
>
> *The SEC-OT focus on controlling attack vectors is in sharp contrast with conventional IT-SEC practices whose focus is on reducing vulnerabilities, such as software defects and firewall misconfigurations.*

SEC-OT seeks primarily to eliminate or tightly control information flows and attack vectors and only secondarily to address remaining residual risks

4

with software-based IT-SEC compensating measures. Chapter 9 explores such compensating measures.

## Key Definitions

The first step in the SEC-OT methodology is to identify which cyber assets must be protected by SEC-OT measures. To this end SEC-OT defines:

---
*Definition*

**Cyber asset** – *any electronic device containing a CPU*

---

Examples of cyber assets include:

• the obvious: cell phones, computers, laptops, PLCs and RTUs,

• less obvious: firewalls, routers and network switches,

• the often ignored: some power tools and intelligent thermostats, and

• the sometimes surprising: USB drives, hard drives, keyboards and mice, all of which contain embedded CPUs and firmware.

SEC-OT also defines:

---
*Definition*

**Industrial control system (ICS)** – *a set of cyber assets that control, or influence the control of, physical industrial operations*

---

A control system is therefore a set of cyber assets that have been grouped together for reasons that make sense to control systems engineers.

---
*Definition*

**Control-critical network** – *a set of one or more ICS networks managed according to SEC-OT principles.*

---

The distinction between ICS networks and control-critical networks is subtle. The ICS definition above is essentially the same as the IEC 62443-1-1 definition of "industrial automation and control system" (IACS)[1]. ICS engineers group assets into control systems for reasons of engineering capability or efficacy.

---

1   *IEC TS 62443-1-1:2009 Industrial communications networks – Network and system security – Part 1-1: Terminology, concepts and models,* International Electrotechnical Commission, 2009

A control-critical network is a *set or group of ICS networks* where the entire set or group is managed according to SEC-OT principles. SEC-OT teams group ICS networks into control-critical groups to facilitate and optimize security. The focus of SEC-OT is preventing attack information from reaching into and compromising control-critical sets of ICS networks by eliminating, limiting and/or controlling both offline and online information flows through the physical and network perimeters of control-critical networks. Chapter 3 describes how to select which ICS networks belong in each control-critical network set.

---

**Note**

*"Control-critical" networks are not the same as "critical-infrastructure" networks. For example, a home appliance manufacturer is not a critical infrastructure in any nation, but the ICS networks in such a manufacturing plant may still be control-critical to the manufacturer.*

---

While SEC-OT is designed to minimize information/attack flows into control-critical networks, large volumes of information typically flow much more freely between the ICS networks inside a control-critical set of networks. SEC-OT's stringent physical protections against information/attack flows apply to communications between the control-critical group and external systems, not between the control systems within the control-critical group.

In principle, a SEC-OT site may define many control-critical networks at an industrial site, each with many component ICS networks. In practice, most SEC-OT sites define a single site-wide control-critical network, containing a single ICS network, at least initially. Such designs help SEC-OT teams focus on their primary mandate: deploying a layer of physical protections to prevent attack information from external sources from reaching any control-critical components.

Many SEC-OT sites, therefore, use the terms "control-critical network," "control network," "critical network," and "industrial control system" interchangeably, having defined a site-wide control-critical network as containing a single ICS. Such sites tend to refer to subsets of this single control network as "zones," "network segments" or "ICS segments."

This book uses terms as defined above, but often abbreviates "control-critical network" as "control network" or "critical network."

When protecting control-critical networks from information/attack flows originating in external networks, SEC-OT observes that there are only two ways to transmit information between cyber assets:

> **Definitions**
>
> ***Offline communications*** *– any mechanism where information is encoded into a physical asset that is moved manually to enable the information to move.*
>
> ***Online communications*** *– any mechanism by which information is transmitted from one cyber asset to another without physically moving an information storage medium.*

For example, USB keys, laptops and floppy disks that are carried from one cyber asset to another are examples of offline communications. Serial connections, Wi-Fi connections and twisted-pair Ethernet all facilitate online communications.

SEC-OT physical protections must address the threat of attacks embedded in both offline and online communications. A variety of physical protections for offline communications are described in Chapter 4. Air gaps and unidirectional gateway technology, which are the only two physical protection mechanisms supported by SEC-OT for online communications with critical networks, are described in Chapters 5 and 6.

## Secure Operations Technology

The SEC-OT perspectives, principles and practices documented in this book are drawn from a decade of working with secure industrial sites, and with other experts who work with such sites.

The key difference between secure industrial sites and non-SEC-OT sites is not the sites' size or industry, but the degree of determination to reduce cyber risks to continuous operations.

> **Note**
>
> *The single most common reason industrial sites transition to the SEC-OT methodology is the sites' need to dramatically reduce cyber risks to continuous operations.*

Industrial enterprises generally adopt SEC-OT principles and practices because the business has decided that IT-SEC protections alone are not sufficient to address cyber threats to continuous, correct and efficient operation of physical, industrial processes.

> **Note**
>
> *SEC-OT pioneers come from a wide range of site sizes and industries, including small electric substations, railway signalling systems, refineries and power plants.*

The Secure Operations Technology methodology can be summarized in five steps:

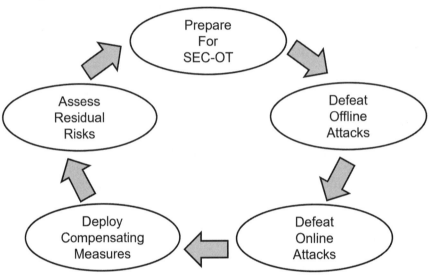

*Figure (1) SEC-OT Methodology*

1. **Prepare for SEC-OT** – Identify cyber assets whose compromise can cause unacceptable physical consequences, arrange them into ICS and control-critical networks and then create inventories of information flows/attack vectors.

2. **Defeat Offline Attacks** – Deploy physical, technological, and procedural protections from removable media, removable devices and other offline information/attack flows into control-critical networks.

3. **Defeat Online Attacks** – Deploy physical, technological, and procedural protections from online information/attacks flowing into control networks.

4. **Deploy Compensating Measures** – Deploy IT-SEC compensating measures and other software-based defences as a second line of defence.

5. **Assess Residual Risks** – Carry out a capabilities-based risk assessment of the resulting SEC-OT design to determine residual risks.

Some practitioners argue that the risk-assessment step should come first in the SEC-OT process to determine whether any change is needed to an existing IT-SEC design. In practice, capabilities-based assessments of IT-SEC designs have little value. Such assessments invariably conclude that IT-SEC designs reliably prevent few unacceptable physical consequences in the face of even unsophisticated attacks.

When transitioning to SEC-OT, few sites adopt all SEC-OT best practices at once. Most sites adopt essential principles and practices in a first phase of deployment and transition to a more comprehensive and mature SEC-OT posture over a course of years. Even after a site is mature in SEC-OT practices, SEC-OT security programs still evolve over time, as new best practices continue to be developed by SEC-OT pioneers.

## This Book

This book is focused on the technical security controls and associated operating policies and principles essential to the SEC-OT methodology. This book does not describe a full security program. Readers who need full program guidance are encouraged to apply the SEC-OT methodology within the context of larger security program advice such as the NIST Framework[2] or the French ANSSI standards for industrial control systems[3,4].

This book is not an introduction to computer programming, operating systems, IP networking, industrial systems, cybersecurity, or industrial cybersecurity. Readers are assumed to be familiar with the basics of these disciplines – terms such as "drivers," "buffer overflow," "three-way handshake," "HMI," "PKI," and "IT/OT interface" are used throughout, without definition or introduction.

## Summary

Secure Operations Technology is a perspective – a way of looking at and understanding security – as well as a methodology, a set of principles and a set of best practices. The key differences between SEC-OT and IT-SEC are:

- SEC-OT: protect physical operations from information/attack flows – do so physically rather than with only software and focus on attack capabilities, not vulnerabilities.

---

2  *Framework for Improving Critical Infrastructure Security, Version 1.1,* National Institute of Standards and Technology, 2018
3  *Cybersecurity for Industrial Control Systems - Classification Method and Key Measures,* Agence nationale de la sécurité des systèmes d'information, 2014
4  *Cybersecurity for Industrial Control Systems – Detailed Measures,* Agence nationale de la sécurité des systèmes d'information, 2014

- IT-SEC: protect information wherever it flows – do so with encryption and security software and focus on reducing device and system vulnerabilities.

To this end, SEC-OT defines control system security as protecting the safe and reliable control of physical operations from attacks embedded in information. Fundamental SEC-OT principles include:

1. Capabilities-based, not vulnerabilities-based risk assessments,

2. Physical, rather than only software protections, and

3. Inventories of and controls over flows of information/attacks into control systems.

The SEC-OT methodology includes five steps and associated sets of best practices: preparation, defeating offline attacks, defeating online attacks, deploying IT-SEC compensating measures and assessing residual risks.

# Chapter 2  Offshore Platform Case Study

This chapter describes an offshore oil and gas platform that adopted the SEC-OT methodology. This example introduces and motivates elements of the methodology.

In the pre-SEC-OT design for the platform, the drilling, production, and ballast control networks were modelled as three industrial control systems. The control systems were managed using an engineering-change-control discipline to evaluate the safety and reliability impacts of all changes before applying those changes to a control system. Platform cybersecurity functions were managed by IT personnel who specialized in ICS cybersecurity. This team applied a mature IT-SEC program to both IT and ICS networks.

Platform management decided to apply the SEC-OT methodology to platform control systems after concluding that software-only protections were insufficient to their needs. A SEC-OT team was tasked with producing a first-phase SEC-OT deployment for the platform.

## IT-SEC Design

The original IT-SEC design for the offshore platform networks is summarized below:

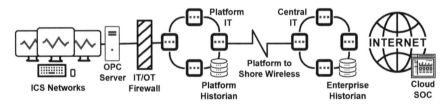

*Figure (2) Original IT-SEC Design*

Details of the original design include:

- On-platform ICS and IT networks,

- The platform IT network connected via leased-frequency wireless communications to an onshore IT network,

- An IT/OT firewall,

- An OPC server configured as an aggregator for information shared across the IT/OT firewall,

11

- A historian database on the platform IT network gathering data from the ICS networks via the ICS OPC server, and

- The security status of all IT and ICS networks managed by an outsourced security operations center (SOC).

Additional facilities configured in the original IT-SEC security program included:

- Communications encryption and authentication functions enabled for all IT network communications including the IT platform-to-shore wireless connection,

- Within the ICS networks, encryption and authentication functions enabled for all ICS components that supported these facilities,

- Role-based access control (RBAC) and per-user passwords enabled on all equipment that supported these functions, with a dedicated ICS Active Directory server controlling access to and for all Windows equipment in the primarily-Windows ICS networks,

- Antivirus systems installed on all IT and ICS equipment whose vendors supported such protections, and

- Additional firewalls limiting the communications permitted between ICS networks (not illustrated).

## Prepare for SEC-OT

The first step of the SEC-OT methodology has the SEC-OT design team classifying cyber assets, grouping those assets into industrial control systems and then grouping the ICS networks into control-critical networks. This was a straightforward process for the mature offshore IT-SEC design:

- The existing ICS networks shared no switches with the IT network.

- The ICS switches and every cyber asset connected to them were classed as control-critical.

- All the ICS networks were grouped into a single control-critical network.

With this classification, it was straightforward to carry out an inventory of both offline and online information/attack flows. Offline flows included:

- USB drives were used routinely on both IT and the control-critical networks and were used to move information between those networks.

- Vendors visiting the site brought their own laptops and connected the laptops to the control network routinely to interact with control-critical cyber assets.

- New computers and replacement equipment, each with a hard drive full of information, were brought to the platform from time to time.

- People physically walked into and out of badged ICS areas.

The IT/OT firewalls rules were then reviewed by the SEC-OT team to produce an inventory of online information/attack flows. Online flows included:

- The platform historian sent queries into the control-critical OPC server every few seconds, and OPC data was returned from those queries.

- The control-network antivirus (AV) server (not illustrated) routinely pulled AV signature updates from the platform AV server.

- The control WSUS server (not illustrated) routinely pulled Windows updates from the corporate WSUS server onshore.

- Files were sent from ICS to IT networks and vice versa, as needed.

- All ICS equipment able to produce Syslog, Windows logs or SNMP traps forwarded that information to the outsourced SOC via the enterprise IT network.

All these information/attack flows needed mitigation in the SEC-OT process.

## Defeat Offline Attacks

The next step of the methodology was to define physical protections for offline information/attack flows.

### *Laptops*

Any laptop that has ever been exposed to an IT network or to the Internet is at risk of compromise by anything from common malware to very sophisticated malware. Some malware can propagate automatically to control-critical networks if a compromised laptop is connected to those networks.

The SEC-OT team for the platform therefore defined a new policy that forbade connecting external laptops to any control-critical network. Every visitor to the control-critical area of the offshore platform who needed a laptop was required to request one before visiting the platform. The visitor provided a list of software that was needed on the laptop and IT personnel provisioned such a laptop from a pool of control-critical laptops. The laptop was configured using known-good media. No control-critical laptop was ever connected to any IT network.

Only these control-critical laptops were permitted by policy to be connected to the any control network or control-critical cyber asset on the platform. The vendor returned the laptop to the control-critical pool after leaving the platform.

### *Removable Media*

All removable media can carry malware as well. Worse, all USB drives contain CPUs and firmware that can become compromised. Unlike laptops though, there are times when bringing new information into control-critical assets is unavoidable. To minimize the use of removable media and USB drives, the SEC-OT team took two steps:

- They deployed an online file transfer mechanism from the control-critical network to the platform IT network. On this platform, as at most industrial sites, almost all routine file transfers are from the control-critical network to an external network, such as the IT network, and not vice versa. This "outbound" file transfer mechanism eliminated most of the need to use removable media.

- For information/attacks, such as new software versions, that needed to come into the control network, the SEC-OT team set up a media cleansing station. This was a computer configured with two antivirus systems. Media containing information destined for the control network was first scanned for common malware by both AV systems. Files that passed the scanning process without alarm were copied to brand new, clearly labelled media that were stored beside the scanning workstation. Only these new media were permitted to be used on the control network.

Most of the new control-critical media remained in the scanning area because the file transfer computer was adjacent to the scanning workstation. Most new media were immediately inserted into the file transfer computer, loaded to the hard drive on that computer and so made available for use within the control-critical network.

Complex files, such as security updates, PDF files and complex configuration updates were tested before deployment using an onshore test bed, as is normal for engineering-change-controlled sites. Removable media ports and devices on some ICS equipment were disabled both physically and by software policy, but not all ports could be disabled.

### New Computers

The SEC-OT team reinforced existing IT-SEC and engineering-change-control policies for new computers and other cyber assets destined for control-critical roles: all new equipment must be provisioned with known-clean media, tested for safe, reliable and correct operation using the onshore test bed, and scanned for known malware and security configuration errors, before shipment to the platform. All such computers were clearly labelled. Once these computers were received on the platform, they were permitted to be connected only to the control-critical network – they were never to be connected, however briefly, to anything but control networks or control-critical cyber assets.

### Training and Awareness

The new policies for control-critical laptops and removable media scanning were incorporated into cybersecurity training and awareness programs for all platform personnel and visitors.

A security assessment 12 months after deployment, though, discovered that USB drives were still being used in ways other than dictated by the training. At times, USB drives were used to transfer files from the control network to the IT network rather than use the online file transfer mechanism. In addition, USB drives that had been exposed to IT networks and Internet-exposed laptops were being used to transfer files within the control-critical networks. Both practices exposed the drives to potential contamination from external sources of information/attacks.

To address these issues, the training program was augmented to emphasize how attacks can be embedded in any information flow, any removable media and any USB device with a CPU. Platform technicians quickly learned to recognize that USB devices could become contaminated by contact with non-ICS computers. The updated training program also reinforced the idea that with the control-system file server in place, removable media was no longer needed for routine file transfers. Training also emphasized that for the small number of control devices for which there was no choice but to update firmware using removable media, such media must be clearly labelled, dedicated to the ICS network and never exposed to IT networks.

## Defeat Online Attacks

The SEC-OT methodology demands physical protection from online information flows entering control-critical networks as well. All firewalls, though, are software, including the IT/OT firewall in the platform's original IT-SEC design. All software has vulnerabilities, the potential for misconfiguration, and, thus, a high potential for compromise. In addition, firewalls forward network traffic from one network to another, and all such traffic may encode attacks.

The IT/OT firewall was, therefore, replaced by a unidirectional gateway as the sole connection between control and IT networks. Unidirectional gateway hardware is physically able to transfer information in only one direction – in this case from the platform control network to the platform IT network. Even if unidirectional gateway software components are compromised, the hardware is physically unable to transmit attacks back into the protected control-critical network.

Unidirectional gateway software does not forward network traffic but makes copies of servers. The unidirectional gateway was deployed with the following server replications enabled:

- The control network OPC server was replicated to the platform IT network and the replica was unidirectionally updated once per second. The platform historian was configured to query the replica OPC server for data rather than the control-critical server.

- The new file transfer server on the control-critical network was replicated to the platform IT network. Any file that was dropped into a "transfer" folder on that server was automatically transferred to the replica file server on the IT network.

- The unidirectional gateway was configured as the destination for all security monitoring information for the control-critical network, including Syslog, SNMP and Windows logs traffic. All the control-critical cyber assets were unidirectionally emulated to the platform IT network, where the replicas reported security information and alerts to the outsourced enterprise SOC.

With the unidirectional gateways in place, IT users and applications were able to interact normally with the unidirectional replicas, querying or polling the replicas for information and receiving the latest real-time data from the replicas in response to those queries. The unidirectional gateway though, prevented any online information/attack flows from reaching platform control networks. The new SEC-OT design is illustrated in Figure (3).

In addition, WSUS and antivirus information/attack flows were converted from online flows into offline flows. WSUS updates were tested first using the onshore test bed and then carried to site when IT personnel visited the site to supervise the application of the security and other software updates. AV updates were tested on the test bed as well, downloaded to the platform

16

IT network daily and carried daily through the scanning workstation to the ICS file server, from which they were transmitted to the ICS AV server for deployment.

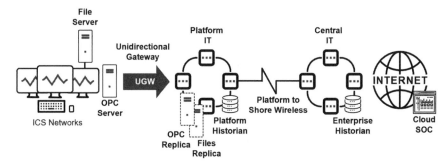

*Figure (3) Initial SEC-OT Design*

### The Turbine Vendor

During the deployment process, it was discovered that platform management had recently committed to a 24x7 monitoring and diagnostics contract with the vendor for the redundant pair of on-platform natural gas turbines that produced electric power for the platform. The vendor was promised a virtual private network (VPN) connection from the vendor's cloud monitoring site, through the Internet, through the enterprise IT network and into the platform's control-critical network so that the vendor would have remote access to the turbine management system servers.

The SEC-OT deployment team determined that this connection posed an unacceptable risk to reliable operations. The vendor's cloud-based management site had VPN connections to hundreds of the vendor's turbines in many countries, with only firewalls proposed to separate these other sites from the vendor's site, and the vendor's site from the offshore-platform control networks. This encrypted, firewalled path through the turbine vendor represented a pivot path for attacks originating from any of the turbine vendor's clients.

The SEC-OT team informed the vendor that they would require the vendor to use the unidirectional gateway instead of the proposed firewalled path for information/attack flows. More specifically:

- The team deployed a turbine-vendor demilitarized zone (DMZ) as the endpoint of the turbine vendor's VPN connection.

- The unidirectional gateway was configured to replicate both turbine management servers from the control network into the turbine-vendor DMZ.

- The turbine vendor would monitor the replicas to determine when the turbines or their management systems needed adjustment.

- When adjustments were needed the vendor would contact platform personnel and use a unidirectional remote screen view mechanism to supervise necessary adjustments.

The unidirectional remote screen view mechanism, when activated, provided a real-time view of turbine management server screens to turbine vendor personnel across the VPN. The vendors could see the screens, but were physically unable to send any command, keystroke or mouse movement through the unidirectional gateway hardware back into the control networks. Platform engineering personnel would receive advice over the phone from the turbine vendor, and when the platform engineers understood and approved the turbine system changes, they would apply those changes under the supervision of the turbine vendors.

The as-built architecture is summarized below:

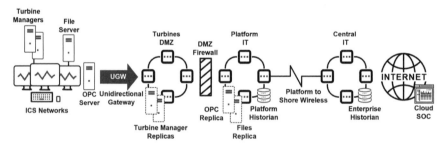

*Figure (4) As-built SEC-OT Design*

All remaining information/attack flows that were online in the IT-SEC design were converted to offline SEC-OT flows:

- Antivirus signature updates were first tested in the onshore test bed to ensure that the updates would not identify any software on control-critical networks as malware and so impair physical operations. The updates were then written daily to a write-once CD by platform personnel and carried through the AV scanning workstation procedure to be transmitted into the control-critical AV server for distribution.

- WSUS updates similarly were tested in depth in the onshore test bed for safe and reliable operation. The updates, once approved by engineering,

18

were again written by platform personnel to a write-once CD and physically carried to the critical network file server via the AV scanning workstation.

## IT-SEC Measures

The remaining IT-SEC protections for ICS networks were not changed by the SEC-OT deployment. ICS passwords and other policies continued to be managed by the critical-network Active Directory (AD) controller, detailed security and other audit records continued to be replicated through the unidirectional gateway to the cloud SOC, and the three ICS networks in the single control-critical network continued to be separated by firewalls (not illustrated).

## Security Posture

The SEC-OT deployment dramatically improved the platform's security posture:

- The SEC-OT project eliminated all online information flows into the platform's control-critical network. No remote-control attack, no matter how sophisticated, can reach into the SEC-OT-protected network and impair critical operations.

- The project eliminated routine USB drive and other removable media use by deploying an online, unidirectional file transfer mechanism from the critical network to the IT network. Training and awareness programs further reduced the transfer of media between critical and noncritical networks, and the scanning station introduced an extra layer of offline protection.

- The SEC-OT project eliminated routine use of external laptops on critical networks.

All these changes were in addition to the existing IT-SEC security measures, which continued unchanged.

Enhancements that the SEC-OT team could consider for future projects include:

- Logically or physically disabling additional USB and removable media ports and upgrading equipment over time to versions and vendors that do not rely on removable media,

- Upgrading critical network switches to support Network Access Control (NAC) so that the accidental connection to control networks of external laptops or other unauthorized cyber assets poses no threat to continuous operations, and

- Enabling alerts for policy violations such as unauthorized attempts to use USB drives and laptops and following up on those alerts promptly.

All these measures represent best practices that are described in greater detail in later chapters.

## Summary

An offshore platform augmented an existing IT-SEC security program for ICS equipment with SEC-OT-recommended physical protections for both offline and online information/attack flows into the platform control systems:

- Risks of offline information/attack flows were addressed by a new "no external laptops" policy, by routing removable media and USB drives through an AV scanning workstation and by testing complex new files, software and configurations for safety and reliability via an onshore test bed.

- High-volume, online information/attack flows were disabled by replicating servers through unidirectional gateway hardware into the platform IT network.

- Lower volume information/attack flows that were online in the IT-SEC design were converted to offline flows in the SEC-OT design.

When the team was notified that platform management had agreed to a remote monitoring and diagnostics contract with the platform's two natural gas power turbines, the SEC-OT plan was updated. The new plan included additional unidirectional replications for the turbine management systems and remote screen viewing for those management systems, so platform engineers could supervise and physically control any changes that turbine vendors recommended.

When a subsequent security assessment revealed that platform personnel were still using USB drives in dangerous ways, training and awareness programs were updated to emphasize the dangers of USB information/attack flows.

In short, the SEC-OT security program physically eliminated all online and most offline information/attack flows into the offshore platform's control system networks, and deployed strong testing, inspection and control procedures and technologies for the remaining offline flows.

# Chapter 3  Prepare for SEC-OT

This chapter describes preliminary steps and decisions essential to preparing for a SEC-OT deployment. These steps include carrying out an inventory of, and classifying cyber assets as, control-critical or not critical, grouping assets into industrial control systems, grouping control systems into control-critical networks, physically separating control-critical assets from noncritical assets, and carrying out an inventory of information/attack flows.

## Classify

Classifying cyber assets establishes a preliminary scope for the SEC-OT process. The goal of classification is to identify the cyber assets that are essential to safe and reliable physical operations. When a team applying SEC-OT has less than site-wide responsibility, the classification step is naturally constrained to only the assets for which the team has responsibility.

Even then, a SEC-OT team may further constrain the set of assets in scope for business reasons, such as seeking to gain experience with SEC-OT on a subset of the control assets at a site, before expanding the scope of the methodology to a larger set of assets.

Asset classification identifies three classes of cyber assets:

- **Control-critical** assets – such as PLCs, RTUs, HMIs, safety systems, protective relays, communications front ends, and their associated switches and routers that are clearly involved in controlling physical processes,

- **IT-centric** assets – such as accounting workstations, sales laptops, customer-facing websites, and their associated switches and routers that should have nothing to do with physical control, and

- **Ambiguous** assets – such as some process historians, site-wide or enterprise-wide optimization systems, and/or control technician tablets, that are difficult to classify.

Ambiguous assets are labelled as such initially and are reclassified in subsequent steps of the methodology.

> **Note**
>
> *All assets at a site that directly control physical operations must be classified as control-critical.*

Asset classification is generally carried out in two phases. An initial assessment is typically based on an asset inventory based on high-level documentation and the recollection of experts in the room during the first-phase SEC-OT planning process. A later, more detailed assessment involves a comprehensive physical inventory of assets at a site and incremental classification of assets discovered by the detailed inventory that were missed in the initial assessment.

The most-thorough sites also consider physical consequences due to potentially unreliable, or improper operation of, external inputs that are essential to safe and reliable industrial operations. Many sites, for example, consider:

- Electric power to the site, which can be interrupted, or can be caused to exceed safe voltage and current levels,

- Natural gas pipelines for heating and other purposes, which can be interrupted, or can be over-pressurized leading to leaks, fires and explosions,

- Air conditioning systems for control system server rooms and other rooms that must be climate-controlled, which can be interrupted,

- Heating, ventilation and air conditioning (HVAC) for areas hosting 24x7 operations staff or other vital personnel, which can be interrupted,

- Uninterruptible power supplies for control-critical assets, which can be disabled, exhausted or over-charged, leading to fires, and

- Water supplies, which can be interrupted or contaminated.

In some cases, the cyber assets controlling these essential physical systems can be brought into scope for the SEC-OT methodology. Other cyber assets are more challenging to manage because they are owned or operated by some other department, enterprise or government agency.

## Group Assets

An industrial control system is defined as a *set* of cyber assets whose worst-case compromise results in unacceptable physical consequences, and a control-critical network is defined as a set of ICS networks. The next step to protecting an ICS is deciding how to group control-critical cyber assets into these sets.

---

**Note**

*All cyber assets identified as control-critical must become part of a control-critical network.*

---

When defining ICS sets, SEC-OT teams seek to group assets with similar functions, communications needs and security needs. When defining control-critical networks, these teams seek to minimize the volume and complexity of information flows into critical networks from noncritical networks. Initial definitions of ICS and control-critical network sets are typically revisited several times in the process of preparing for a SEC-OT design effort as information/attack flows are analyzed.

In practice, many SEC-OT sites initially define only one control-critical network per site and one ICS in that control-critical network. Such a design minimizes the number of ICS network perimeters that will require physical protection from offline and online information/attack flows.

> **Note**
>
> *SEC-OT demands physical segmentation and protection of control-critical networks from noncritical networks.*
>
> *Firewalls and other software segmentation may be used between the ICS members of a control-critical network, but not between a control-critical network and any other network.*

The most common exception to the "one control-critical network per site" rule of thumb is an exception for safety-instrumented systems (SIS). SEC-OT teams occasionally group SIS networks into one or more small control-critical networks separate from the main control-critical network at the site. Such networks are often referred to as "safety-critical" networks. All safety-critical networks are also control-critical networks.

A less common exception to the "one critical-network" rule of thumb is for protective relays. Such relays are cyber assets that prevent damage to electrical equipment. When a control-critical network contains only protective relays and associated support assets, that network is often referred to as an "equipment-critical" network. All equipment-critical networks are also control-critical.

## Physical Segmentation
With tentative groupings in place, SEC-OT practitioners design their networks to physically separate each control-critical network from all external networks. This physical separation is a prerequisite for physical protection. Physical separation means:

• Cyber assets in a control-critical network are not connected to the same physical switch, VLAN-enabled or not, as are IT assets, assets from a different control-critical network, or any noncritical assets, and

- Virtual cyber assets in one control network do not run as guests on the same physical server as IT assets, assets from a different control-critical network, or other noncritical assets.

When this physical segmentation results in significant re-cabling of control system networks, SEC-OT teams may revisit their initial asset classification or control system groupings. Reducing wiring changes for existing installations is one of the reasons that many sites define only a single control-critical network for the entire site. Such a definition permits the team to use VLANs and firewalls to separate ICS subnetworks of a control-critical network rather than physically separate the subnetworks.

SEC-OT teams also routinely reclassify small numbers of IT cyber assets as control-critical assets in order to leave those assets on the same physical switch as the control system.

> **Note**
>
> *All cyber assets in a control-critical network must be managed as control-critical assets per the SEC-OT methodology.*

More specifically – an IT asset left in a control-critical network for convenience of wiring becomes a control-critical asset and must be managed as a critical asset in the SEC-OT methodology.

> **Note**
>
> *When practical, SEC-OT sites locate IT and ICS assets in different server rooms.*

Additional physical separation, where practical, simplifies certain physical protection mechanisms. For example, separate control-critical and IT server rooms allow industrial sites to issue access badges for the IT room to IT personnel, for the control-critical room to ICS personnel, and not vice versa. Such separation also reduces opportunities for errors and omissions that might otherwise result in physical cross-connections between control-critical and noncritical network wiring and equipment.

## Information/Attack Flows

With a tentative plan in place for the physical separation of control systems from other systems, a SEC-OT team can start considering all information flows – both offline and online – that bring information/attacks into control-critical networks.

An initial version of the survey is often carried out on a whiteboard, from the memory of experts in the room or from an examination of existing firewall rules. A more comprehensive survey is generally carried out later in the SEC-OT process to confirm this initial assessment. The comprehensive survey may inspect as-built documentation, physical devices and wiring, firewall rules, control system software configurations and other sources.

With initial segmentation and an inventory of control-critical perimeter-crossing information/attack flows in place, the team can start the process of revisiting assets whose classification was initially ambiguous.

> **Note**
>
> *The goal of critical-network definition is to minimize the volume and frequency of communicating information/attacks into control-critical networks.*

It is often possible for SEC-OT teams to reduce information flows into critical networks by carefully defining the criticality of cyber assets and occasionally moving an asset from one network to another.

For example, if a conventional operator HMI workstation was physically connected to an IT network, the SEC-OT team would observe that the HMI was sending commands into control-critical equipment every few seconds. Reclassifying the HMI workstation as a control-critical asset and moving the workstation from the IT to the control-critical network eliminates the HMI's cross-perimeter traffic into the control-critical network and introduces no new cross-perimeter flows.

In another example, an Enterprise Resource Planning (ERP) system located in the IT network of a chemicals business might send a small number of production orders to the main control-critical network every few hours or days. That ERP, however, exchanges large amounts of information with suppliers, banks and other Internet-based systems. Reclassifying the ERP as an ICS asset would dramatically increase the amount of information/attacks flowing into the control-critical network, not reduce those flows.

> **Note**
>
> *The unidirectional reference architectures in Chapter 6 can further reduce cross-perimeter information/attack flows into control-critical networks.*

While the goal of minimizing information/attack flows into ICS networks applies to both offline and online communications:

> **Note**
>
> *SEC-OT regards most online communications into control-critical networks as higher risk than offline communications – wherever practical, SEC-OT prefers offline communications.*

Online information flows allow attackers to attempt attacks whenever the attackers wish and for as long as they wish. Offline information moves only intermittently, at the whim of the person, truck or pigeon physically carrying the information, dramatically slowing the attack process. Once assets have been grouped into control-critical networks with an inventory of information/attack flows into ICS networks, SEC-OT practitioners can select whether given flows will be implemented via offline or online means. Such practitioners prefer offline flows wherever practical.

Issues of online vs. offline practicality include:

- Required latency – online communications are almost always lower latency than offline communications, but not all communications require low latency.

- Capital versus operating costs – online communications incur technology and labour costs to establish, maintain and manage, while offline communications incur ongoing labour costs. The labour cost of offline communications depends directly on the frequency with which such communications are needed.

- Errors and omissions – offline communications are sometimes less accurate than high-frequency, automated communications, but the calculation is more ambiguous for low-frequency communications. For rare communications, automated online paths may fall into disuse and disrepair between transmissions, increasing their errors and omissions rate.

For example, at SEC-OT sites:

- Security updates are generally communicated manually into ICS test beds, and from test beds into control-critical networks. Most sites conclude that the small manual effort needed to write updates to a CD and carry the CD across a perimeter is not worth automating, given the extensive and time-consuming testing those updates must subsequently undergo before deployment.

- Second-by-second commands from a power grid control center to a power plant to produce more or less energy are communicated via online communications.

- Daily antivirus (AV) updates are communicated manually via offline mechanisms at some sites, and online at others.

SEC-OT teams rearrange network boundaries to minimize all information/attack flows entering a network and minimize online information/attack flows in particular.

## Summary

Preliminary steps in the SEC-OT methodology include:

- Carrying out a physical inventory of cyber assets at the industrial site and classification of each asset as control-critical, IT-centric or "ambiguous, where all equipment able to physically control industrial processes must be classified as control-critical,

- Grouping control-critical cyber assets into industrial control systems,

- Grouping industrial control systems into control-critical networks,

- Separating control-critical networks from other networks physically rather than with only software,

- Carrying out a comprehensive inventory of information/attack flows from external systems into control-critical networks,

- Reclassifying ambiguous cyber assets to minimize information/attack flows into ICS networks, and

- Rendering a decision for each information/attack flow as to whether to use offline or online mechanisms for the flow.

Physical separation sometimes extends to situating IT and ICS assets in separate server rooms.

# Chapter 4  Defeat Offline Attacks

To defeat offline attacks, the SEC-OT team carries out an inventory of all offline information/attack flows into ICS networks and then addresses the risks of such flows using a variety of techniques. This chapter reviews commonly-applied offline information/attack flows and their remediation.

## Offline Survey

All offline attacks are physically transported into industrial sites. Offline information/attack flows at most sites include:

* Removable media,

* Removable devices, such as vendor laptops, cell phones and USB drives,

* New permanent computers,

* People – who carry information in their heads and may have malicious intent, and

* Exotic attacks – shipments of physical products, such as structural steel, that might hide wireless scanners and attack tools, as well as automobiles, trucks, drones, remote-controlled robots and other intrinsically mobile computing platforms.

Information and attacks arriving from "trusted suppliers" can be particularly deceiving.

---
**Note**

*That a supplier is considered trustworthy does not mean that all the supplier's employees, contractors and suppliers are trustworthy.*

*That a person is considered trustworthy does not mean that all the data that person carries is trustworthy.*

---

## Test Beds

A control-system test bed is an important tool for inspecting and testing offline information flows. Most industrial sites already have access to at a laboratory that contains at least "one of each" kind of ICS cyber asset, software and version in use at the site sites. Ideally there is an accurate copy of each industrial control system available for testing – the more accurate the copy, the more useful the copy is for testing proposed changes.

Most industrial sites already use their test beds to test new versions of software, security updates and other complex information artifacts for at least safety and reliability, before deploying these information artifacts on a live control system.

SEC-OT sites add security testing to the goal of the ICS test bed. An ideal test bed is:

* As accurate a representation of the industrial control system as possible,

* Thoroughly instrumented to enable testing for safety and reliability, and

* Thoroughly instrumented for security.

When new software versions, updates, complex configuration changes or other complex information/attack artifacts are candidates for deployment on an ICS network, those candidates are first tested on the test bed. The test bed is instrumented and operated to determine whether the new software correctly handles normal ICS operating conditions as well as a wide variety of upset conditions, including safety shutdowns and other emergency conditions.

The test bed is also instrumented for security, in much the same way as commercial anti-malware "sandbox" products are instrumented: allow the clock to move faster or slower into the future, test for the creation of unexpected files and network connections and look for other behaviours that differ from what is normal for the test bed. Security and performance monitoring sensors for the test bed are generally set to a very high level of sensitivity. This produces a high rate of false positive alarms, all of which must be investigated, but SEC-OT sites would rather use the test bed to thoroughly understand the behaviour of new information artifacts than see those artifacts deployed on a live control system without such understanding.

Test beds must not be connected to live control-critical networks by firewalls or other software artifacts. If an attack compromises a test bed as a result of some inbound information flow, that attack must have no physical means of propagating to the live control system.

Most often ICS test beds are part of IT networks. IT and Internet connectivity can simplify the detection of malware that connects to Internet-based command and control centers. A risk with such connectivity though, is that targeted malware can be programmed to shut down and betray no symptoms on the test bed when the malware detects Internet connectivity. The malware uses the fact that the test bed is Internet-connected, and the knowledge that no control-critical network is even Internet-connected, to hide from the test bed's security sensors.

A less common but more thorough design connects the ICS test bed unidirectionally to the IT network, in the same way as a production ICS network is connected. Unidirectional gateways may also be used to emulate live ICS data sources to the test bed in order to make the test bed a more realistic emulation of the live ICS, for testing the safety, reliability and security characteristics of new information artifacts. Unidirectional gateways and unidirectional network reference architectures are discussed in Chapters 5 and 6.

## Removable Media

Removable media are the source of many compromises of non-SEC-OT networks by common, high-volume malware and ransomware. SEC-OT defines removable media as:

> **Definition**
>
> **Removable media** – any mechanism for information storage that does not contain a CPU

> **Note**
>
> By this definition USB devices are not removable media because all such devices contain a CPU.

For example, CDs, DVDs, magnetic tapes and floppy disks are removable media, but USB hard drives, solid state drives and flash drives are not. All USB devices contain CPUs and so must be treated as removable devices. By this definition, pieces of paper are removable media as well, particularly when the contents of such papers are electronically scanned into control system equipment.

To deal with removable media, SEC-OT sites generally implement security controls that include:

- Operating system and application software policy changes that forbid mounting removable media on control-critical cyber assets and raise alerts when mount attempts are detected,

- Anti-malware scanning computers or kiosks,

- Physical protection, disabling or removal of removable media hardware and connectivity mechanisms from critical assets, and

- A security near-miss protocol analogous to the U.S. Occupational Safety and Health Administration (OSHA) safety near-miss protocol.

Each control is discussed in detail below.

### Automated Policies

Microsoft Windows Active Directory servers can be configured to apply a security policy to all managed Windows computers, instructing those computers to refuse to mount removable media, or refuse such mounts to all but privileged users on special machines. Denying all removable media mounting is preferred at SEC-OT sites – that a site trusts certain users does not mean the site should trust the contents of those users' CDs.

Individual Linux computers can be similarly configured, but forbidding the "root" administrative account from mounting removable media is very difficult. Preventing such mounts on industrial devices can be equally difficult or impossible, depending on which operating system the dedicated devices use. Even on Windows machines, sophisticated attackers with physical access to the machines can often find ways to defeat Active Directory permissions. Nonetheless, SEC-OT sites use software policies and derive what protection is possible from software.

Software policies are also configured to report all attempts to mount removable media, whether successful or not. These alerts are generally transmitted in real time to a central SOC. When security analysts at the SOC sees these alerts, the analysts correlate the alerts with open work orders. Any alerts outside the scope of approved work orders trigger at least a phone call to the affected site and result in either an incident response escalation or a near-miss report as described below.

### Anti-Malware Scanning Stations

SEC-OT sites routinely deploy anti-malware scanning workstations or kiosks at the security desks or badged doors that are the physical security boundary of control-critical networks. A scanner/kiosk is one or more physical computers running one or more anti-malware scanning engines. Roll-your-own installations may use multiple computers with as many scanning engines running simultaneously on each computer as can coexist – multiple anti-malware engines frequently do not coexist well on a single computer. Commercial multi-scanning solutions generally require only a single scanning computer or "kiosk" and are typically configured with between four and eight anti-malware scanning engines.

Multi-scanning solutions generally have a user interface that shows users the files on their media, allows users to select the files to scan, and then writes the scanned files to brand new physical media taken from a dispenser beside the kiosk. The new media are then carried to a nearby file server, which is the only device on the control-critical network with removable media mounting hardware and software enabled. The files are read into the file server and then transferred electronically to the critical network from the file server.

### Physical Protection

SEC-OT sites physically disable or eliminate removable media readers on as much control-critical equipment as is practical, excepting only the file servers adjacent to scanning workstations and kiosks. At many sites however, some low-level PLCs, RTUs and other equipment require the use of removable media or USB drives to update firmware or carry out other routine maintenance. Such sites deploy physical locks on any remaining media readers with manual procedures to authorize, prepare for and follow up on operations that involve unlocking the devices.

These sites colour-code or otherwise label very prominently all physical media that is produced by the scanning stations. Workers at the site are trained that such control-critical media must never leave the control-critical area at the industrial site and must never be inserted into a noncritical computer or laptop. Any such insertion risks writing new attack information to the media. Leaving the site with such media and bringing it back to the site later poses the risk that someone may have inserted the media into a distant, unmonitored computer and deliberately or inadvertently written malicious information to the media.

The goal of these procedures is to provide a reasonably strong assurance that any media inserted into ICS equipment is free of common malware.

### Near Miss Protocol

The US Occupational Safety and Health Administration (OSHA) defines a near miss as:

---

**Definition**

**Near miss** – an incident in which no property was damaged,
and no personal injury was sustained
but where, given a slight shift in time or position,
damage or injury easily could have occurred

---

When potentially-compromised media or cyber assets are connected to control-critical components in violation of procedures that minimize the risk of compromise, such connections are a threat to safe and reliable operations. SEC-OT sites define incidents that could have compromised control-critical networks, but did not, as "cyber near misses."

Establishing a cyber near-miss program analogous to widely-used OSHA programs increases the visibility of removable media and device mistakes. An OSHA-inspired system of reviewing, prioritizing and remediating near misses involves both individual contributors and managers and, over time, nearly eliminates the erroneous use of unauthorized removable media on control-critical networks.

### Inspecting Contents

Anti-malware scanning is only one form of inspection for removable media contents. In addition to such scanning, manual inspection of files entering control-critical networks is preferred at SEC-OT sites. Such inspection is practical for short, high-level, abstract instructions such as "Schedule pumps A, B and C to start at 2 AM every morning, to help minimize electric power costs."

Manual inspection is generally not practical for software updates, new antivirus signatures or new control recipes that contain a schedule of hundreds or thousands of digital and analog values paired with cryptically-named devices and device registers. SEC-OT sites generally require that these complex information/attack artifacts be deployed first into test beds, not directly from IT networks into live ICS networks. These complex files are first tested in the heavily-instrumented test bed before they are moved into the live ICS.

## Removable Devices

Removable devices are a threat as serious as removable media:

> **Definition**
>
> **Removable device** – any cyber asset with temporary online access to a control-critical cyber asset

By this definition, all laptops, cell phones and USB devices are removable devices. Even modern hard drives, keyboards and mice frequently contain CPUs and firmware. Removable device CPUs communicate with connected ICS cyber assets, however temporarily. The risk with such connections is that a removable device running attack software, however inadvertently, can launch active attacks against software in all connected cyber assets.

> **Note**
>
> *SEC-OT sites generally forbid connecting external removable devices to any ICS asset.*

When SEC-OT sites need portable computers and other removable devices on the ICS network, the sites address this need in standard ways:

- **Vendor laptops:** When vendors require access to certain software tools on a laptop at a SEC-OT site, the vendor requests such a laptop from the site before the visit. The site provisions a control-critical laptop with known-good media and makes the laptop available to the vendor during the visit. This laptop is never connected to noncritical networks, and no vendor laptop or other external laptop is ever permitted to connect to critical networks.

- **Network Access Control (NAC):** To help enforce the "no external laptops" rule, many SEC-OT sites enable Network Access Control on their ICS networks. NAC is software protection and so is not proof against sophisticated attacks but is sufficient to block, and alarm on, accidental connections by vendor laptops.

- **Alerts:** All SEC-OT sites enable alerts for connections to unauthorized removable devices to the greatest extent practical, including unauthorized USB drives, keyboards and mice. Such alerts are generally routed to a central SOC. SOC analysts investigate the alerts and trigger either incident investigations or near-miss reports.

- **Contracts:** Whenever practical, vendor contracts include penalties for unauthorized connections of any kind of removable device to any kind of control-critical cyber asset.

- **Labelling:** Control-critical assets and network connections are clearly labelled, and unused network and other removable device connectors are physically blocked to prevent mistaken connections.

- **USB chargers:** Some SEC-OT sites have programs to easily request, provision and maintain USB charging stations throughout the site, to reduce the temptation to subvert physical blocks and charge cell phones or other portable noncritical equipment from control-critical equipment USB ports.

Again, these provisions are applied to all removable devices, including USB mice and keyboards. Such devices are not permitted temporary connections to control-critical equipment. When USB mice, keyboards or other devices are required on critical networks, the devices are first tested on the relevant ICS test bed, labelled as control-critical equipment and permanently assigned to the critical network, as described in the section "New Cyber Assets" below.

> **Note**
>
> *Unauthorized wireless access points are singularly dangerous removable devices.*

Rogue access points, if permitted to operate, provide a path for attack information to bypass some of the physical protections on which SEC-OT sites rely. Well-meaning technicians and vendors may expect that they can routinely attach such equipment to critical networks, at least temporarily. Preventing such attachments is a high priority for SEC-OT personnel, vendor training and awareness programs, as well as NAC and near-miss programs.

## Encrypted USB Drives

SEC-OT sites generally avoid USB drive encryption systems. Vendors of such systems maintain that encryption makes the control-critical drives unrecognizable on IT networks and vice versa, so that cross-contamination is impossible. SEC-OT sites distrust such claims because:

- Encrypting drive contents does not address the risk of malware compromising USB drive firmware, and every removable drive contains a CPU and firmware,

- All cryptosystems are software and can be hacked, and

- Relying on software to protect control-critical computers rather than strict alerting and near-miss protocols makes users complacent in the use of USB drives. This increases the opportunity for sophisticated, firmware-based attacks at the affected sites.

## New Cyber Assets

New and replacement cyber assets are introduced into all control-critical networks from time to time, with occasional bulk additions of new assets when control systems are upgraded or expanded. When new cyber assets are being prepared for use on a critical network, whether those assets be USB mice, laptops, displays or servers, the assets must be inspected and tested to ensure that they do not contain embedded attack information.

The problem with inspection is that modern devices are complex and often packaged to defeat inspection. Dismantling most hard drives, flash drives or monitors to thoroughly inspect their circuit boards, for example, generally destroys the device being inspected. Even for equipment where inspection is possible, circuit boards in laptops and servers can be very complex and beyond the means of most sites to inspect.

SEC-OT sites currently take all the following measures to assure the integrity of new cyber assets entering a control-critical network.

- **Test bed:** All new cyber assets destined for control-critical networks are first deployed on the safety, reliability, and security test bed and monitored closely throughout functional and security tests.

- **Consumables:** Commodity "consumable" types of equipment that are difficult to inspect physically, such as keyboards and mice, are purchased from unpredictable vendors. This way, the new equipment may still contain common, high-volume attacks, but is much less likely to contain the most sophisticated attacks that are targeted at a specific SEC-OT site.

- **Inspection:** When inspection is possible, the contents of new cyber assets are compared to vendor schematics, photographs of similar equipment, and purchasing information, to determine whether delivered circuit boards and chipsets match vendor specifications and whether unwanted hardware components, especially wireless communications components, have been delivered as part of the new equipment.

- **Contracts:** Whenever practical, hardware and systems integration contracts include penalties for delivering equipment that contains unauthorized hardware, especially additional CPUs, firmware or wireless communications hardware. Such penalty clauses increase the motivation for product and service providers to include supply chain integrity measures in their own purchasing and handling procedures.

- **Labelling:** Control-critical cyber assets are clearly labelled as such, and site personnel are trained never to connect noncritical assets to control-critical networks and vice versa.

Most SEC-OT sites maintain an inventory of pretested control-critical cyber assets that can be deployed to address emergency hardware failures. When ICS assets are decommissioned, their labelling is removed, and the assets are erased and reprovisioned for use outside the critical network, or physically destroyed, or first erased and then destroyed.

The greater question of cyber risks due to new cyber assets is the subject of ongoing "supply chain integrity" research in the ICS security community.

## Insider Attacks

Insiders with physical access to critical cyber assets are a perennial concern at SEC-OT sites as well as non-SEC-OT sites. SEC-OT sites apply as many of the usual personnel precautions as are permitted by local privacy and other laws, including:

- **Auditing:** Enable detailed auditing of local and remote user actions on all control-system assets as a deterrent to deliberate misoperation.

- **Forensics:** Write these audit records and other records through a unidirectional gateway into a physically tamper-proof forensic repository.

- **Video monitoring:** Deploy video monitoring and recording, to help associate malicious insiders to forensic records.

- **Investigations:** Use forensic records and video recordings routinely and visibly in routine safety and security near-miss investigations – monitoring is a deterrent only when potential perpetrators know that they are being monitored.

- **Personnel surety program:** Deploy a comprehensive program for evaluating insider risks, for example including periodic background checks for criminal convictions and other indicators of risk, psychological profiling and periodic employee interviews.

The above is only a summary. SEC-OT sites routinely draw from subdisciplines of personnel security in conventional physical security and IT-SEC domains.

## Deceived Insiders

Even well-meaning insiders carry information into control-critical sites, networks and cyber assets. Sometimes this information is a physical object such as a cell phone or USB drive – the risks posed by these physical objects are addressed by the measures described earlier in this chapter. Sometimes though, the attack information flows through the minds of insiders – if an attacker can persuade an insider to act on false information, there can be physical consequences.

SEC-OT sites train their insiders to be suspicious of all information received from outside of control-critical networks, including information that may appear to have originated in the critical network, but which has travelled through a noncritical network and is therefore no longer as trustworthy as information that has never left the critical network.

> **Note**
>
> *SEC-OT sites must take care to avoid creating animosity between ICS, IT, and vendor personnel. That ICS personnel must be suspicious of externally-sourced information and advice does not mean that the people providing such advice or maintaining external systems are incompetent or malicious.*

It is external networks, cyber assets and any information potentially contaminated by contact with noncritical assets that are suspect – not capable and well-intentioned IT or vendor colleagues.

The most difficult part of training ICS personnel to suspect external devices and information is not the principles, but the practice of identifying data sources that are more open to tampering than SEC-OT-protected sources.

For example, a site may replicate an ICS historian unidirectionally to an IT network. This replica could then supply data to a web application whose output is available on the cell phones of ICS personnel. The cell phone app may have the same look and feel as other critical-network ICS applications from the same vendor. This familiarity does not mean that the information provided by the cell phone app is safe – information received by the app has traversed both an IT network and the Internet and may have been compromised in transit.

ICS personnel must be trained to verify externally-acquired information, before transferring that information to ICS assets or physically acting on the information. This includes:

* **Important instructions in email** – including instructions that appear to be from their supervisor or another credible authority – such instructions should be verified verbally with the source authority, and

* **Optimization advice or settings** – provided by external applications or that traverse an external network before reaching the ICS personnel. This includes any advice received wirelessly. Such settings, instructions and advice should always be verified against internal ICS status and measurements before acting on the advice, to ensure that the advice will not cause unacceptable physical consequences when applied to physical equipment.

It is often easier to train site personnel with a "whitelist" of acceptable sources of information than try to explain data flows in enough detail for people to determine for themselves which data is trustworthy and which requires verification from control-critical sources.

## Nonessential Equipment

Some equipment on control-critical networks does not need to run continuously. All such equipment should be configured to shut down automatically when idle.

For example, shutting down the engineering workstations used to program, test and manage ICS networks and especially SIS networks is very important. The same is true of laptops the site keeps in stock for visiting vendors. Such workstations and laptops are often populated with copies of powerful tools that can manipulate, reconfigure and reprogram live control equipment. Even with SEC-OT-recommended physical protections against cyber compromise, best practice dictates keeping these powerful tools password-protected and turned off until needed.

## Exotic Attacks

Attack information that is physically shipped into industrial sites becomes a threat only if that information becomes available to a control-critical cyber asset. For example, a hexadecimal rendering of a ransomware executable printed on the side of a steel girder entering a site is a threat only if that code is somehow scanned and converted into a form that can be executed.

A more credible threat is when cyber assets enter a site surreptitiously, especially those with wireless communications capabilities. For example, a battery-operated Wi-Fi scanner taped to the side of a steel girder that reports discovered Wi-Fi networks at the site through a cellular connection to an attacker is a credible threat. Threats like these are one of many reasons SEC-OT sites generally disable all Wi-Fi connections to control-critical networks. Note that a compromised cell phone in the pocket of an employee at the site poses the same threat as the scanner taped to the girder – both can discover and remotely attack control-critical Wi-Fi networks.

A comparatively new threat vector is intrinsically mobile cyber assets that enter a site. Drones can carry physical assaults into a site, as well as Wi-Fi sniffers and attack tools. Modern automobiles contain over 100 CPUs each, many of which are accessible via Wi-Fi, Bluetooth, cellular or other wireless connections. The compromise of a cyber asset in an automobile or truck at a site can result in significant casualties and physical damage to the site.

Some of these threats can be mitigated by limiting wireless networks at the site to unidirectionally-protected, monitor-only functions as described in the Wireless Networks reference architecture in Chapter 6. Others are the subject of active debate, research and SEC-OT best-practice development.

## Summary

The only way for a control-critical network to change from an uncompromised to a compromised state is if attack information passes into the network via offline or online means. A survey of offline information flows reveals all possible offline cyber attack vectors.

An ICS test bed is an essential SEC-OT tool for testing complex incoming information such as antivirus signatures, security updates and new software versions. Such a test bed should be as accurate a copy of the live ICS systems at a site as is practical. These test beds should be thoroughly instrumented and monitored for safety, reliability and security issues.

At most sites, offline attack vectors and protections include:

- **Removable Media:** Deploy anti-malware scanning kiosks and workstations to test media entering a site. Physically disable removable media ports. Configure control-critical components to report alerts when media are used anywhere else and manage these alerts using a near-miss process.

- **Removable Devices:** Ban vendor laptops, USB drives and other external computers from connecting to control-critical hosts and networks. Physically disable removable device ports, such as unused network and USB ports. Configure control-critical networks and cyber assets to raise alerts when unauthorized connections are attempted and manage these alerts using a near-miss process. Deploy known-clean control-critical laptops provisioned with required software for visiting vendors and other personnel who need the equipment.

- **New Cyber Assets:** Deploy all new equipment first on the test bed and test the equipment for safety, reliability and security.

- **Insider Attacks:** Deploy detailed auditing and surveillance. Use these tools routinely in security and safety near-miss remediation.

- **Deceived Insiders:** Teach ICS personnel to trust only control-critical equipment. All instructions, setpoints and monitoring information received via other means – such as cell phone apps and electronic mail – should be verified against trustworthy sources before acting on the information in a way that might have unacceptable physical consequences.

- **Nonessential Equipment:** Turn off nonessential equipment when not in use, especially ICS laptops and engineering workstations.

- **Exotic Attacks:** Some exotic attacks can be mitigated by the Wireless Networks reference architecture. Others are the subject of active research, debate and best-practice development.

# Chapter 5  Defeat Online Attacks

To defeat online attacks, the SEC-OT team carries out an inventory of all online information/attack flows into ICS networks and then addresses the risks of such flows using unidirectional gateways primarily, and air gaps more rarely.

Air gaps and unidirectional gateway technology are the only two physical boundary protection mechanisms supported by SEC-OT as protection against information/attack flows into control-critical networks from external networks. Firewalls may be used in series with unidirectional gateways and for internal segmentation within control-critical networks, but not as primary perimeter protection – firewalls are software protection, not physical protection from information/attack flows.

This chapter introduces and gives examples of both unidirectional gateways and air gaps. Chapter 6 provides a comprehensive catalogue of unidirectional network reference architectures, including architectures that may seem counter-intuitive, such as those providing vendor remote access, central engineering teams and continuous high-level control of industrial sites from external authorities.

## Online Survey

At industrial sites with ICS firewalls already deployed, a preliminary inventory of information flows can be as simple as reviewing existing firewall rules. Online information flows often include:

- IT client connections to ICS databases, historians and even monitoring and control devices to acquire operations data that supports business decision making,

- OT equipment connecting to IT infrastructure servers such as Active Directory, DNS, AV and WSUS servers,

- Control-critical equipment connected to vendor monitoring and update sites via modems and the Internet,

- IP and serial connections to wireless LAN and WAN infrastructure, including leased-frequency microwave communications, and

- Interactive remote access connections to permit systems integrators, product vendors, IT personnel, management and others unrestricted access to control-critical equipment.

A more comprehensive inventory often includes a physical inspection of

43

the ICS site to detect undocumented firewalls, wireless routers, modems and other online connections to control-critical equipment.

## Air Gaps

**Definition**

***Air gapped network*** *– any set of cyber assets with no means of online communications with any external assets*

For at least thirty years, industrial control systems have seen steadily increased connectivity. Air gaps have become increasingly rare. Examples of air gaps at modern SEC-OT sites include Safety Instrumented Systems (SIS) and LED displays on portable tools. Air gaps are frequently criticized though:

- Air gaps impede the movement of valuable status monitoring information out of control systems and into enterprise applications, and

- Air gaps impede the movement of security monitoring information that is increasingly seen as essential to assessing equipment status and assessing the strength of security postures.

In the cases where air gaps are still practical, however, such gaps represent the most thorough possible physical protection from online cyber attacks.

**Note**

*The term "air gap" is frequently used in a cavalier fashion by stakeholders not familiar with their control systems' as-built designs.*

Security assessors routinely report finding many "unexpected" connections to control systems that were described as air-gapped. When converting a site to SEC-OT methodology, any claims that existing equipment is air-gapped should be verified by a physical inspection of the affected equipment, its associated cabling and any possible wireless interfaces. Where practical, an inspection of network communications within air-gapped networks can be valuable as well – packets that are received from or sent to cyber assets outside of the air-gapped network can indicate online connections outside of the network.

## Unidirectional Gateways

> **Definition**
>
> **Unidirectional gateway** – a combination of hardware and software. The hardware is physically able to send information in only one direction and the software replicates servers and emulates devices

Unidirectional gateways are essential to SEC-OT in any environment where impaired industrial production is an unacceptable consequence. The most common deployment of such gateways is at the IT/OT interface, where the gateway can transmit monitoring data out of a control-critical network without the ability to send any information or attacks back into the system from the IT network.

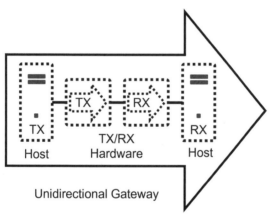

*Figure (5) Unidirectional Gateway Internals*

The most robust unidirectional hardware design consists of a fiber-optic transmitter connected to a fiber-optic receiver with a short piece of fiber-optic cabling. The receiver in such designs has no laser, and so is physically unable to send any information or attack back to the transmitter. The transmitter has no photo cell or fiber-optic receiver able to receive a signal, even if one were sent.

With this type of physical protection in place, it does not matter if the software components of a unidirectional gateway are compromised – no software compromise can impair the ability of the gateway to physically prevent online attacks from reaching the transmitting network.

> **Note**
>
> *Unidirectional gateways of varying quality are available from a variety of vendors. The best equipment uses unidirectional optical signalling described above and is certified as unidirectional by an accredited Common Criteria laboratory or its equivalent.*

Unidirectional gateway software replicates servers and emulates devices. For example, a gateway may be deployed to replicate a historian server or other database from a control system to an IT network. The replica database is a normal part of the IT network. IT users and applications requiring real-time data interact normally with the IT replica database, sending the replica queries and receiving as responses the same data that the ICS database would have provided.

In another example, a unidirectional gateway may be deployed to emulate an OPC-UA server from a control system to an IT network. The gateway polls the control-system OPC-UA server periodically and sends snapshots of control-system state information unidirectionally to the IT network. In the IT network, the unidirectional gateway implements a second OPC-UA server. This replica OPC server is a normal part of the IT network. IT users and applications requiring real-time data interact normally with the emulated OPC-UA server on the IT network, sending poll requests to the replica and receiving as responses the same data as the ICS server would have provided.

> **Note**
>
> *Common questions about unidirectional gateways include "how can they negotiate a TCP 3-way handshake?" and "why replicate servers?"*
>
> *Unidirectional gateways are not routers – they never forward network traffic from one network to another.*
> *Instead, the gateways are endpoints of TCP connections on source and destination networks.*

Unidirectional gateways forward device state information from one or more devices on a source network to one or more replicas on a destination network. Queries from the destination network are sent to the replicas. Unidirectional gateways, by design, cannot forward polls and queries into protected networks.

The TCP connections from unidirectional gateways to networks on either side of the gateways are independent connections and often exchange very different kinds of packets. For example, a gateway configured for database replication would send queries to the source database on the ICS network and would send "insert" and "update" commands to the replica database on the external network.

---

**Note**

*Another common question is "What happens if the IT replica is attacked, corrupted, and the corrupted information is used to make decisions – can this process misoperate the ICS?"*

*Incorrect decisions can be made from business network replicas, but to control the physical process, such decisions must be communicated somehow back into the ICS.*

---

The offline protections in Chapter 4 address such potentially-compromised information/attack flows, especially the section "Deceived Insiders."

## Network Layers

IT-SEC defence in depth advice recommends many layers of software protection for ICS sites as protection from online attacks originating on IT networks and the Internet. Layers of firewalls and networks are one kind of layered defence that defence-in-depth recommends – usually a minimum of the following, depending on the source of guidance:

- An Internet firewall between the Internet and an IT DMZ network

- A DMZ firewall between the DMZ and the IT network

- An IT/OT firewall between the IT network and an ICS DMZ,

- An ICS DMZ firewall between the ICS DMZ and the ICS plant-wide network,

- Production unit firewalls between the plant-wide network and individual DCS, SCADA, or production cell controllers,

- Device network firewalls between production units and their networks of connected PLCs, and

- A SCADA WAN firewall between a SCADA system and the WAN that connects the system to remote sites and equipment.

IT-SEC best practice recommends that no two layers of firewalls be sourced from the same vendor, in hopes that no single vendor's firewall vulnerability can be used to traverse multiple layers in this defensive structure.

This design has many intrinsic limitations, which is why SEC-OT practitioners prefer physical protections, such as air gaps and unidirectional gateways, to firewalls and other software protections. The IT-SEC design is not fundamentally flawed however – SEC-OT sites still tend to arrange their networks this way, with one key difference:

> **Note**
>
> *SEC-OT sites generally deploy unidirectional gateways to replace or augment at least one complete layer of firewalls in an IT-SEC defence-in-depth architecture.*

One complete layer of unidirectional protection between the Internet and the control devices that directly control physical operations is sufficient to prevent online attacks from pivoting through firewalls and intervening networks to misoperate the physical process.

More generally, SEC-OT sites use unidirectional gateways to separate control-critical networks from noncritical networks. Noncritical networks always include:

• The Internet,

• IT networks, through which Internet-based attacks often pivot into ICS targets, and

• Any wireless network, since wireless communications are intrinsically broadcast, and it is impossible to which nearby wireless devices have access to the wireless communications.

Wide-area networks, such as SCADA WANs, are most often modelled as non-control-critical networks, since, by definition, WAN communications extend outside of any physical security perimeter controlled by the industrial site. There are exceptions to this rule though, discussed in Chapter 6.

Test bed networks are most often considered non-control-critical as well. The most thorough test-beds though, are provided with most of the same physical protections against information/attack flows as control-critical networks, to make the test-beds faithful emulations of such networks.

Chapter 6 explores a wide variety of unidirectional network reference architectures that increase the strength of IT-SEC defence-in-depth designs to SEC-OT standards.

## Summary

Air gaps and unidirectional gateways are the only physical protections that SEC-OT endorses to defeat online attacks from noncritical networks reliably.

- Air gaps permit no online information/attack flows at all, and

- Unidirectional gateways are a combination of hardware and software – the hardware is physically able to transmit information in only one direction, and the software replicates servers and emulates devices.

Unidirectionally-replicated databases and emulated devices are normal participants in IT networks. Users query the replicas and receive the same answers from the replicas those queries would have produced from the original ICS databases and servers.

Unidirectional gateways are most commonly oriented to send information from a control-critical network to external networks and physically permit no information/attack flows back into the critical network. Unidirectional gateways are most commonly deployed to completely replace one layer of firewalls in a defence in depth, layered network architecture.

SEC-OT sites use firewalls extensively within control-critical networks and between ICS networks in the same control-critical groups but not between critical and noncritical networks.

# Chapter 6  Unidirectional Architectures

This chapter documents unidirectional network reference architectures that are used routinely in SEC-OT network designs.

> **Note**
>
> *SEC-OT practitioners are cautioned that most unidirectional gateway vendors support only a subset of these patterns without costly custom engineering.*

SEC-OT pioneers continue to invent new patterns for new ICS applications and needs.

## Database Replication

Database replication is one of the most common reference architectures. Most ICS networks are designed to simplify application integration by concentrating operations information in a small number of data repositories such as Microsoft SQL Server databases or process historians.

In the database replication architecture, a replica database is established on the enterprise IT network and a unidirectional gateway copies the contents of an industrial database in a control-critical network to the enterprise replica. Enterprise users and applications access the replica normally.

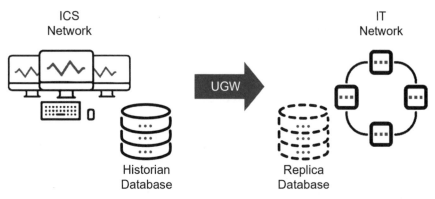

*Figure (6) Unidirectional Database Replication*

The replica may be local, in an IT network at the industrial site, or may be remote, typically at a head-office data center or other central site. A local replica at the industrial site reduces latency and other communications costs for applications on the site's IT network that make intensive use of industrial data. A central enterprise database aggregating data from many

51

industrial sites provides an industrial enterprise with an information resource that can be used to compare performance and other details between industrial sites. SEC-OT businesses may use local replicas, central enterprise databases, or both.

> **Note**
>
> *When replica databases develop gaps, for example due to scheduled downtime to apply security updates to unidirectional gateway components, those gaps can be repaired by manually triggering the retransmission of data from the source database.*

Retransmitting data to fill historical gaps is called "back-filling" the replica database. The back-fill process retransmits data from the industrial database and populates missing records into the replica database, without duplicating any records that already exist there. The process is generally triggered manually from the industrial network. Less commonly, the process is carried out regularly and automatically, for example a daily retransmission of all the previous day's data. Such regular, programmed retransmissions though, increase network and other resource utilization.

> **Note**
>
> *Practitioners not familiar with unidirectional gateways sometimes ask how they can send queries from an IT application, through a gateway, into an industrial database.*
>
> *Database replication means no such queries ever need to be sent – queries from IT users are sent to the IT replica database, which answers such queries normally.*

This is the essence of database replication. Source databases are normal parts of control system networks and respond normally to queries and commands from ICS equipment and users. Replica databases are normal parts of IT networks and respond normally to queries and commands from IT applications and users.

Database replication is one of the most common unidirectional network architectures and is used in a wide variety of industries. For example:

- Historian databases are replicated routinely from ICS to IT networks in many industries, including: electric power generation and transmission, offshore platforms, oil and gas pipelines, refining, chemical and pharmaceuticals, and water and wastewater treatment.

- Relational databases are replicated routinely to IT networks in railway signalling and Industrial Internet of Things (IIoT) applications.

- Proprietary, real-time databases are replicated routinely to IT networks and vendor cloud systems in vendor monitoring and predictive maintenance applications.

An extra feature of some database replications is meta-data replication. When new tables, points or tags are added to source databases on industrial networks, some unidirectional gateways can automatically propagate those new data sources to the replica databases. This feature, when available and enabled, reduces database maintenance costs by reducing data entry costs for the replica database.

## Device Emulation

When no industrial database is deployed on a control-critical network, or when software licensing costs or other considerations make replication of such a database undesirable, SEC-OT sites may elect to emulate industrial devices to the IT network. A unidirectional gateway typically polls communications servers or devices directly, using device protocols such as OPC-UA, Modbus or Siemens S7. The gateway transmits device state snapshots to the IT network where the gateway emulates the industrial devices to the IT network. IT applications, such as IT databases and historians, access the emulated replicas as if those replicas were the original industrial devices.

---

**Note**

*Practitioners not familiar with unidirectional gateways sometimes ask how they can send poll requests through the gateways from an IT application into an industrial device.*

*Device emulation means no such polls need be sent through a gateway – poll requests are sent to the IT replicas, which answer those requests as the original devices would have.*

---

For example, an enterprise may decide to deploy a single enterprise historian at a head office rather than a plant historian at every site. SEC-OT teams then deploy unidirectional gateways to emulate ICS devices or OPC servers to the IT network to provide data to the enterprise historian.

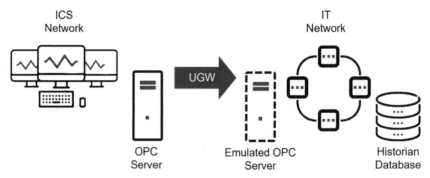

*Figure (7) OPC Server Emulation*

With device emulation however, there is often no "back-fill" function possible. This is because most industrial protocols have no way to ask a device for data that the device observed in the past. When a complete record of device readings is essential in central database, SEC-OT sites generally either:

- Deploy a high-availability unidirectional gateway, one that is tolerant of single points of failure, thus preventing gaps from appearing in enterprise databases,

- Deploy a short-term historian at the industrial site, recording all the data in all the devices at the site, so that if a gap develops in the enterprise historian, that gap can be back-filled manually from the short-term historian, or

- Replicate a database instead of emulating a device.

Device emulation is sometimes referred to as "protocol emulation." The term is not entirely accurate but does provide insight into how the reference architecture can be applied. Device emulation can be used to emulate many kinds of servers that use "protocols," including:

- Publish/subscribe messaging endpoints,

- Video surveillance cameras,

- Network printers, and

- Network time servers.

These emulations are in addition to a wide variety of PLCs, RTUs and other industrial devices and OPC servers.

## Application Replication

Many control systems include HMIs, web servers and other sophisticated applications that are difficult to replicate or emulate. Instead, unidirectional gateways are deployed routinely to replicate the relational databases, historians, OPC servers and other data sources that serve data to ICS applications. A second instance of the sophisticated application is then deployed on the IT network. The ICS instance serves critical-network users, and the IT instance serves IT and sometimes Internet-based users.

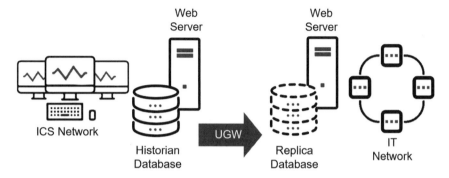

*Figure (8) ICS Web Server Access via Database Replication*

In many cases, these applications also store configurations, images or other supporting information in files. SEC-OT sites often deploy file server replication for the folders containing these files so that when configuration changes are made to the ICS application, such as adding new web pages or editing HMI screens, those changes propagate automatically to the IT instance of the application. Such replication reduces management costs for the replica application.

## Remote Diagnostics and Maintenance

ICS product vendors are experts as to the operation, trouble-shooting and maintenance of their physical and/or software products. Increasingly, such vendors offer remote diagnostic and maintenance services for their products. Such offerings may be very attractive to industrial sites, especially to those sites and organizations too small to maintain their own expert-level personnel for every important technology used at their sites.

The Remote Diagnostics and Maintenance reference architecture enables remote diagnostic and maintenance services for unidirectionally-protected control-critical networks. In this architecture, a unidirectional gateway replicates industrial databases or devices to an IT network or DMZ. Vendors connect to the replicas using VPN connections, as if the replicas were the original industrial systems. Vendors and their expert/analysis software systems use the unidirectional replicas to draw conclusions about when the vendors' products at an industrial site need service or adjustment.

When a vendor sees an opportunity to improve a product through remote adjustment, they contact the customer site and schedule a remote screen view session. At the scheduled time, an engineer with access to the control-critical network at the site calls the vendor over the phone and activates remote screen view. Remote screen view sends real-time images of the screen of a cyber asset through a unidirectional gateway to a web server on the IT network or a DMZ. The remote vendor connects a browser to the web server to see the screens but cannot send any command, mouse movement or attack back through the gateway into the control network.

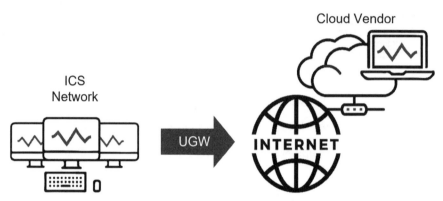

*Figure (9) Unidirectional Remote Screen View*

The vendor provides instructions over the phone to the engineer at the site. The engineer works with the vendor to understand the problem and the proposed solution. Only when the engineer understands both, does she apply the vendor's recommended corrective actions.

The vendor interprets this process as supervising site personnel in the application of a complex correction to the vendor's products at the site. The engineer at the site interprets the process as supervising the vendor. Both perspectives are legitimate, and both sets of needs are met by this approach to remote support, without the risks that come from firewalled remote access.

An additional advantage of this approach to remote support is that vendor personnel do not need to be screened and trained for every site they service, as would be the case if these vendors had been given unescorted remote access to the site.

This Remote Diagnostics and Maintenance reference architecture is applied routinely to electric power turbines and less commonly to a wide variety of other hardware and software systems.

## Emergency Maintenance

In an emergency, a qualified engineer may not be available with access to control-critical networks to operate a remote screen view session. To support emergency maintenance requests, SEC-OT sites may deploy emergency access hardware. This hardware is typically a network appliance with two twisted-pair Ethernet interfaces and a physical key or keypad on the front panel. In an emergency, personnel at the site contact their support providers. Those providers advise site personnel to go to their key closet, sign out the key for the emergency access hardware, insert the key in the access hardware and activate the hardware.

This physical process engages the access hardware function and physically connects two copper or optical cables inside the device, temporarily enabling bidirectional communications with a control-critical network. The emergency access device has a built-in timer. When the timer expires, or when electric power to the device is lost, the device automatically and physically disconnects the cables again.

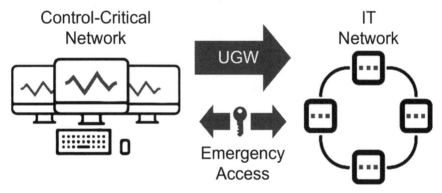

*Figure (10) Emergency Maintenance*

The access unit is typically deployed in parallel with a unidirectional gateway and in serial with a conventional firewall/VPN server, jump host and/or other IT-SEC remote access mechanisms. In normal usage, the control-critical network is physically, unidirectionally protected. For the duration of a declared emergency at the site, the emergency access unit temporarily enables a software-protected remote access path into the control-critical network.

> **Note**
>
> *Most SEC-OT sites prefer remote screen view to emergency access hardware, because unidirectional hardware protection for the control-critical network is preserved during remote screen view sessions but not during emergency access sessions.*

Most hardware and software vendors, though, prefer the Emergency Maintenance reference architecture to the Remote Diagnostics and Maintenance architecture. With the Emergency Maintenance architecture, vendors can do what they wish to systems at a remote site without explaining anything to site personnel. Some SEC-OT sites acquiesce to vendor demands and provide remote access via the Emergency Maintenance architecture. Other sites explain to their vendors that if the vendors are not prepared to provide their remote support services securely, the site will need to cancel the support agreement and pay some other service provider for remote diagnostics and maintenance. Vendors frequently accommodate sites who phrase the choice this way.

## Continuous Remote Operation

Some industrial sites require continuous or nearly-continuous remote control from another site. For example, a tank farm storing oil for an oil pipeline might have an operator 8x5 but shift off-hours control to a 24x7 pipeline operator at a central site. In another example, some industrial sites do not have engineers on site and rely on a central engineering or IT team. These central teams generally have one or more people connected remotely, continuously to every industrial site in the enterprise. Neither the Remote Maintenance and Diagnostics nor the Emergency Maintenance architecture is appropriate to these continuous, long-term connectivity needs.

At such sites, SEC-OT practitioners define a control-critical WAN that contains all the equipment, local and remote, that can control a given industrial process. In the tank farm example, the tank farm control systems and pipeline control systems form a single control-critical network. In the central engineering example, all the managed plants as well as the central engineering office are modelled as a single control-critical network. Private telecommunications capacity is used to connect the distributed sites, not public switched networks. Firewalls and site-to-site VPNs are deployed at every site's interface to the private WAN.

SEC-OT permits firewalls in the connection to the private WAN because the entire WAN is modelled as a single control-critical network. In this instance, the firewalls represent internal network segmentation, not an interface to an external, noncritical network.

This means though, that all the component sites in this critical WAN must be protected as thoroughly as the most sensitive of the connected sites is protected. For example, if any of the connected industrial sites has "guards, gates and guns," so must every site, including the central engineering office. This also means that physical, unidirectional protections against information/attack flows from external networks must be deployed at the interface between any part of this extended control-critical WAN and any noncritical network such as an IT network or the Internet.

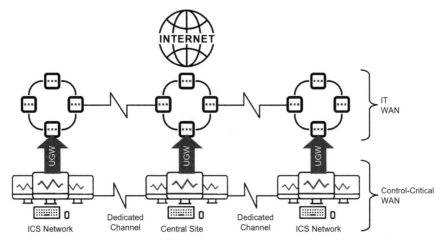

*Figure (11) Continuous Remote Operation via Control-Critical WAN*

In this architecture, unidirectional gateways may be deployed centrally, at a large site or an engineering office, or may be deployed at each industrial site that is part of the critical WAN. Most businesses prefer to deploy the gateways at a central site with 24x7 engineering staff, but this may increase telecommunications costs when all communications must be routed through the central site.

The decision whether to deploy gateways at each site vs. centrally is a business decision, not a security decision, provided that the entire control-critical WAN is managed as a SEC-OT network, not an IT network.

## Device Data Sniffing

Test and training systems can benefit from access to live data feeds rather than simulated sources. Normally, the Database Replication and Device Emulation architectures are sufficient to provide such data unidirectionally into test beds, without risk to control-critical networks. In some cases, though, ICS systems or devices cannot tolerate the unidirectional gateway sending additional queries in order to replicate the systems.

For example, some control and monitoring devices support only one TCP connection at a time to a central control system, and so cannot be queried by both the control system and a unidirectional gateway serving the test bed. In another example, some WAN connections to monitoring and control devices are low-bandwidth and cannot tolerate doubling network traffic – one set of traffic to send live values to the control system and another to send values to the gateway serving the test system.

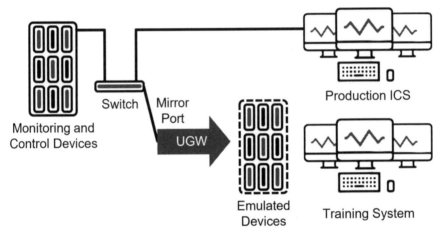

*Figure (12) Device Data Sniffing for a Test and Training System*

The Device Data Sniffing reference architecture addresses these needs. A unidirectional gateway is connected to one or more mirror ports on the ICS switches through which device communications pass. Special gateway software examines the replicated traffic captures and extracts device values from those captures so that the ICS devices can be emulated to the test network. The unidirectional gateways then respond to queries from the test bed using the values observed in device-to-control-system communications. This architecture enables emulating devices to a test bed without new connections to those devices and without increasing network traffic to the devices.

The Device Data Sniffing reference architecture is used most commonly in electric power transmission and distribution networks, where hundreds of limited-functionality remote RTUs may be accessible only via costly, low-speed, leased telecommunications capacity.

## Central or Cloud SOC

Most enterprises have a central security operations center (SOC) rather than a SOC at each industrial site. Increasingly, central SOCs are hosted by a third-party cloud provider, and may be staffed by that provider's experts. Central SOCs have many benefits, not least that they can gather and correlate information from many industrial and IT sites to determine whether and what kind of attacks might be in progress.

ICS Network                          WAN          Central SOC

*Figure (13) Central or Cloud SOC*

Unidirectional gateways are deployed routinely to enable central monitoring by emulating Syslog devices, SNMP clients, log file servers and other security-relevant devices into central monitoring sites. This architecture enables central monitoring of security conditions in control-critical networks without introducing the attack paths back into the monitored equipment that firewalled SOC connectivity would introduce.

## Network Intrusion Detection Systems

Unidirectional protections are deployed routinely to enable both signature-based and anomaly-based network intrusion detection systems (NIDS). The gateways replicate traffic captures from SPAN and mirror ports on ICS switches to intrusion detection sensors. Using a unidirectional gateway for this function allows the IDS sensor to be deployed safely on an IT network.

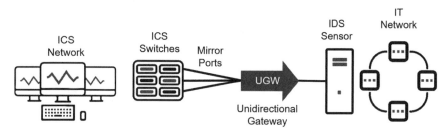

*Figure (14) ICS IDS Sensor Deployed on IT Network*

Connecting the IDS sensor to the IT network is an advantage because most IDS sensors need frequent adjustment, which is typically carried out remotely by security analysts in a central SOC. Deploying a

61

unidirectionally-fed IDS on the IT network makes such remote adjustment straightforward for IT-based SOCs, without introducing the risk of an attack pivoting from the IT network, through a NIDS sensor, into the monitored control-critical network.

> **Note**
>
> *Many switch vendors document their SPAN and mirror ports as unidirectional. Such documentation is often inaccurate.*

Worse, any unidirectional assurances on the part of network switch vendors are software assurances – a stolen password or other compromise of switch software can quickly reconfigure a SPAN or mirror port to support bidirectional communications with the potential to transmit attacks into monitored networks.

An additional benefit of deploying unidirectionally-fed NIDS sensors on IT networks is that, in the event of an upset condition on an ICS network, IDS sensors can sometimes generate large volumes of alert traffic. Some ICS networks are very sensitive to changes in traffic volumes and these bursts of alerts destined for a central SOC can pose a threat to correct operations of the ICS. Deploying the NIDS sensor on the IT network ensures that alert traffic traverses the IT network exclusively, with no impact to operations.

## Convenient File Transfer

SEC-OT sites frequently replicate file servers from control-critical networks to IT networks to facilitate ad-hoc file transfers. Replicating an ICS file server allows ICS technicians to drag and drop files to a folder on the ICS network and have those files appear automatically on a replica IT file server a few moments later.

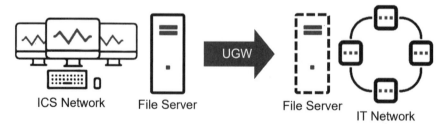

ICS Network    File Server          File Server
                                                IT Network

*Figure (15) File Server Replication*

At most sites, almost all ad-hoc file transfer needs are for transfers from the ICS network to the IT network. At such sites, replicating a file server from the ICS network to the IT network dramatically reduces any need to use removable media or transient devices. Chapter 4 discussed more comprehensive physical protections for offline threats due to removable media and removable devices.

## IIoT and Cloud Communications

The Industrial Internet of Things (IIoT) is a catch-phrase for dramatically increased connectivity for control-critical cyber assets or "edge devices." Such connectivity generally enables:

* The flow of information from edge devices at an industrial site into Internet-based cloud services for "big data analysis,"

* Automatic updates of firmware in edge devices, and occasionally

* Information/attack flows returning to edge devices to control the devices and/or physical infrastructure.

SEC-OT sites have two ways to respond to these requirements:

* Edge devices that monitor physical operations but are physically incapable of controlling those operations can be deployed on their own networks. These networks may be connected directly or wirelessly to IT network segments at the plant or connected directly or indirectly to cellular and Internet networks. Sites with such mixed networks must take care to label IT and ICS cabling and other communications components carefully and prominently to prevent accidental cross-connections at the site.

* Edge devices that control physical operations are control-critical assets and must be deployed and managed using SEC-OT best practices. These assets may be deployed on a main ICS network, on their own ICS network that is part of a control-critical group of ICS networks, or as a separate control-critical network.

A unidirectional gateway is generally deployed to gather information from these edge devices and possibly other systems in a control-critical network, translate the information to Internet/cloud friendly formats, and send the information across the Internet to a cloud service.

When edge devices are part of a control-critical network, software updates must be applied by an IIoT update server that is part of the control-critical network, not applied directly from the cloud. SEC-OT permits no automatic mechanism to send information as complex and potentially dangerous as a firmware update into a control-critical network automatically, without first testing that artifact and verifying its safety, reliability and security characteristics on an ICS test bed.

When information/attack flows must return from the cloud to act on physical equipment, SEC-OT sites inspect and control those flows thoroughly. Most commonly, such inbound information is very abstract, such as a message saying, "equipment X will fail shortly – schedule downtime and send a work crew as soon as possible." Such information is sent to the people responsible for a work process, who inspect the information to make sure it is safe, and then manually apply the new knowledge to the industrial process – for example: by manually scheduling process downtime.

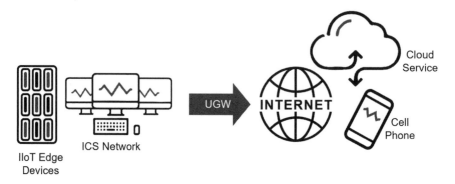

*Figure (16) Cloud Communications*

Continuous, detailed control from an Internet-based cloud is not permitted for control-critical networks. For example, some vendors sell cloud-based HMI services, where remote operators connect through the Internet and send detailed, second-by-second instructions to complex, powerful, and dangerous industrial sites all over the world. Such connectivity is forbidden by SEC-OT.

## Electronic Mail and Web Browsing

Plant operators and other control system personnel at SEC-OT sites frequently need access to corporate electronic mail systems and sometimes Internet web browsing. Such activities are never permitted on control-critical networks. Instead, SEC-OT sites deploy one or more IT-managed computers and screens at 24x7 operator workstations.

Operators can see the IT equipment as part of their array of displays and can use the IT equipment and services as needed. The IT equipment, however, is connected to an IT network and managed as an IT resource, not a control-critical resource.

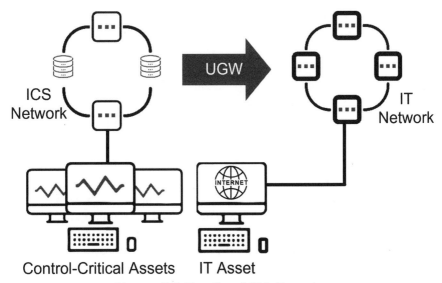

*Figure (17) Email and Web Browsing*

## Partial Replication Protecting Trade Secrets

Some industrial sites may have trade secrets embedded in their industrial systems. A pharmaceutical plant for example, may have batch recipe information embedded in a process historian database, preferring to store this sensitive information exclusively in their physically-protected control-critical network rather than in IT networks.

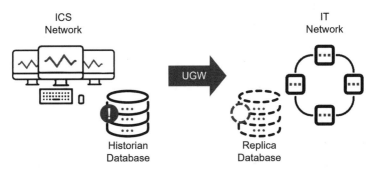

*Figure (18) Partial Replication*

At such sites it is important to configure unidirectional gateways that replicate information out of control-critical networks in a manner that avoids replicating trade secrets. The most common way to do this is to replicate only a subset of information from each ICS server and device to the site's IT network.

The partial replication may select data to replicate by specifying a list of data source names to replicate exclusively, by replicating an entire data source except for a list of names to exclude from replication, or to segregate trade secret information into separate servers and data sources entirely. Complete separation is practical in only some cases. Selecting between a list of names to replicate versus a list of names to exclude from global replication depends on the length of each kind of list of data names and each site's tolerance for errors and omissions in the maintenance of these lists.

## Scheduled Updates

Many industrial sites require scheduled updates of some types of information, such as batch production orders and antivirus updates. Some sites adopt a daily, manual process for such updates – burning the updates to a CD, carrying the CD through the offline protections documented in Chapter 4 and deploying the updates on a test bed. On the test bed, the updates are tested for safety, reliability and security impacts and are ultimately carried into the control system.

Other sites deploy a reversible unidirectional gateway[5] to automate these processes.

### *Reversible Unidirectional Gateways*

A reversible gateway is a unidirectional gateway that replicates servers across one-way hardware, but the hardware can reverse orientation. The hardware can send data one way into a control network, or one way out of such a network, but never both at the same time. The gateway-reversing function can be triggered by a manual input such as a physical button, a key or a touchpad on the front panel of the device, or can be triggered automatically on a schedule. When the schedule is controlled by a CPU in the reversible gateway, that CPU must be air-gapped and blind to any data traversing the device. If this orientation-scheduling CPU can receive no information from either control-critical or IT networks, the CPU cannot be compromised by either network.

When reversible gateways are deployed as the sole connection between a control-critical network and an IT network, the delivery of data from the control network to the IT network is delayed while the gateway is oriented into the control network, and vice versa. When such delays are unacceptable to business users, the reversible gateway may be deployed in

---

5    At this writing the only reversible unidirectional gateway on the market is Waterfall Security Solutions' FLIP

parallel with a conventional "always-on" unidirectional gateway as illustrated in Figure (19).

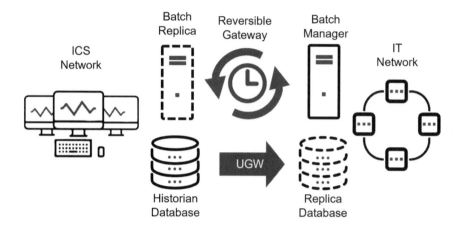

*Figure (19) Reversible Gateway and Conventional Gateway in Parallel*

### Reversible Gateway Security

The degree of security provided by reversible unidirectional gateways is comparable to the security provided by the offline removable media controls described in Chapter 4. Like offline information/attack flows, information through a reversible gateway does not move when the attacker needs the attack information to move but moves when the gateway reverses orientation on a schedule, or because of physical intervention at the site.

A half-duplex communications medium that reverses orientation only a small number of times per day dramatically impairs the command-response capabilities of online, remote-control attacks. Prompt command-response capabilities are essential to the Remote Access Trojan (RAT) malware that attackers prefer to use for high-consequence attacks.

Reversible gateways are most often configured as clients of both control-critical and IT networks, not servers to those networks, and not as routers that forward network traffic. When the time comes to reverse orientation, the gateway software actively fetches batch orders, AV signatures or other content from an authoritative source on an IT network. The gateway verifies the authenticity of this content as well, both in the external IT network and again on the internal network. Configuration as a client rather than a server or router further reduces remote-control attack communications opportunities.

> **Note**
>
> *Unlike firewalls and routers, reversible unidirectional gateways do not forward application protocol requests in one direction and replies in the other.*
>
> *Instead, they replicate one type of server into a control-critical network, and a different type back out to IT networks. Applications on either side of the gateway interact normally with their respective servers or replicas.*

The most cautious SEC-OT sites using reversible gateways also use firewalls to separate the network segment hosting servers that are replicated *from* the IT network from the network segment hosting servers that are replicated *to* the IT network. This makes it even more difficult for attackers to find any round-trip mechanism that might permit command/response round-trip communications of any sort.

## Safety Systems

Some SEC-OT sites unidirectionally segment safety systems from their control networks. When SEC-OT sites do this, it is generally because they:

- Conclude that safety systems are very important control systems and so warrant a second level of unidirectional protection, or

- Conclude that safety systems are comparatively simpler than larger control systems to protect unidirectionally, and so deploy SEC-OT physical protections for safety networks first in a series of progressive deployments of SEC-OT designs and best practices.

Syslog and SNMP clients are routinely replicated unidirectionally from safety networks to SOCs and network operations centers (NOCs), while the safety devices are emulated to ICS networks. ICS network integration permits detailed safety system status information to be represented in general-purpose ICS HMI displays. Plant operators often prefer to integrate safety system alarms and indicators into their primary HMI rather than monitor a second HMI containing only safety information.

In some cases, operators must occasionally send a small number of online commands into safety systems, such as "reset" commands to restore normal operations when safety issues are resolved. The most common way to meet this need is to deploy a small safety-critical HMI console as part of the 24x7 operator workstation, with that console physically wired into the safety-critical network. Operators can see the status of safety systems on their main HMI but can issue control commands to the safety system only via the dedicated safety HMI keyboard and mouse.

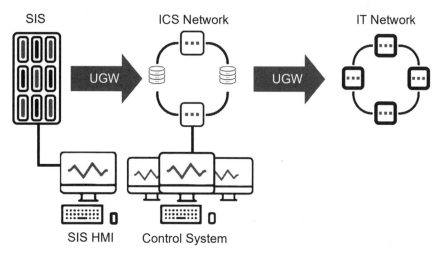

*Figure (20) Integrated SIS Display with Separate SIS Control Computer*

## Continuous High-Level Control

Some sites require very limited continuous remote control from an external source, such as a customer or regulatory authority. For example, electric power plants often require second-by-second instructions from a generating dispatch center that dictates how much power the plant should produce, reflecting the constantly-changing power demands of an electric grid.

In such cases, two unidirectional gateways are deployed. An "outbound" gateway replicates control-critical servers unidirectionally to an external IT or other communications network, while an "inbound" gateway replicates the external control system back into the critical network.

> ### Note
>
> *An inbound/outbound gateway that sends arbitrary queries through one unidirectional path and forwards responses to those queries back through the other path is not a gateway but a forbidden firewall or router.*
>
> *Unidirectional gateways do not forward packets. Gateways replicate servers and emulate devices.*

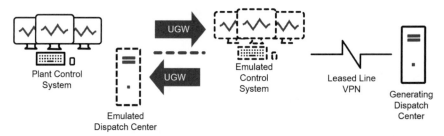

*Figure (21) Power Plant with Continuous Control from Dispatch Center*

Like the reversible unidirectional gateway, inbound/outbound gateway designs are stronger than firewalls:

- Unidirectional gateways do not forward network traffic from one network to another, and so cannot forward the content of attack packets from an external network into a control-critical network.

- Compromising a software component that communicates through a firewall is a one-step process – the attacker finds and exploits a software vulnerability in that software component by sending attack packets through the firewall. Compromising ICS software through a unidirectional gateway that is oriented into a control-critical network is at least a three-step process: first compromise the external host running the server replication software using one vulnerability or exploit, then compromise the internal gateway host with a different vulnerability and exploit, and then do the same again to an ICS component inside the ICS network.

This last step of compromising an ICS component must be carried out "blind" – without feedback of any sort to the attacker. This is because neither the inbound nor outbound unidirectional gateways forward network traffic. There is, therefore, no kind of network traffic that RAT attack code can generate that will result in feedback returning to the external attacker.

Compromising the control-critical network by attacking through an inward-oriented unidirectional gateway is a realistic threat only when there are ICS insiders deliberately cooperating with the remote attackers. The insiders must provide the attackers with detailed information about the progress of the attack, the design of the control-critical network and the configuration of ICS components. The attack is more credible when ICS insiders actively assist the attackers. In-person assistance is essential to this type of online attack, because the attackers are otherwise blind to the progress of their attack and the nature of the ICS network they are attacking.

70

Sites deploying the Continuous High-Level Control reference architecture tend to prioritize the deployment of insider threat management systems documented in Chapter 4 as well.

## SCADA WAN

WANs are intrinsic parts of SCADA systems – SCADA systems must communicate across a WAN to distant and often unstaffed locations such as pumping stations, compressor stations, electric substations and wind turbines. The most robust design for SCADA systems observes that elements of the SCADA WAN reside outside of any site's physical security perimeter and so cannot be modelled as part of a control-critical network. Instead, each remote site and the central site are modelled as their own critical network, with unidirectional gateways at interfaces to the SCADA WAN.

Most often, the central site must be able to both monitor remote sites and control them – for example: turn pumps and compressors on and off, open and close switches or valves and activate, deactivate or tune wind turbines. This means that unidirectionally-protected remote sites use the Continuous High-Level Control reference architecture at their interfaces to the SCADA WAN. In that architecture, unidirectional gateways emulate the central SCADA system to each remote site so that equipment at the site can interact with the local replica as if the replica were the original SCADA system, and vice versa – emulate site equipment to the central SCADA system.

*Figure (22) Remote Site with Continuous Control from SCADA System*

When remote sites are distant from support staff, the ability to carry out some kinds of remote maintenance is advantageous. In practice, only a fraction of maintenance issues can be resolved remotely – for example, when physical equipment malfunctions there is generally no alternative to dispatching a repair crew to replace the failed component. Still, reducing the number of times that crews must be dispatched reduces costs.

To facilitate remote cyber maintenance, one or more maintenance workstations are generally deployed at the central SCADA site, and unidirectional gateways replicate maintenance information and requests from these workstations into remote sites. Maintenance commands from these workstations though, are generally not arbitrary commands with unknown consequences.

Instead, remote maintenance is typically managed by a workflow mechanism. Permitted remote maintenance actions for each station are enumerated and only short identifiers, such as small integers, are communicated to each remote station to activate maintenance actions. When these commands arrive at a remote station, the unidirectional gateway checks to ensure that the numbered actions exist and then triggers predefined actions, such as the execution of numbered scripts or batch files.

In many SCADA installations, some remote sites are more valuable or more consequential than others. Enterprises may initially deploy the full SEC-OT methodology at their most important remote sites and only a subset of SEC-OT practices at lesser sites. Such enterprises lease dedicated, private network capacity to their remote sites and protect the most valuable sites unidirectionally with the "Continuous High-Level Control" architecture and maintenance systems described above. Less-valuable and less-consequential sites use software protection – most commonly including encrypting firewalls.

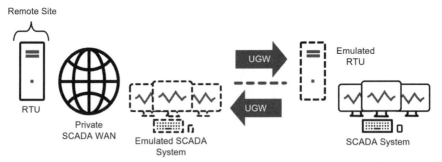

*Figure (23) Software-Protected Remote Site with Continuous Control*

## Protective Relays

Protective relays are deployed to protect electrical equipment from damaging conditions such as lightning strikes, ground faults, overheating and overloading. Most commonly such relays are deployed in high-voltage substations distributed throughout a large geography. Because of their role in preventing damage to costly equipment, protective relays are generally regarded as very important to the reliability of industrial sites.

Some SEC-OT sites therefore choose to deploy SEC-OT best practices for their protective relays, even if the utility is not yet ready to deploy physical protections for other equipment. For example, electric transmission utilities sometimes deploy two Ethernet switches in each of their high-voltage substations: one switch hosting the equipment-critical protective relay network and the other hosting monitoring and control equipment for non-protective functions such as high-voltage power switches and capacitor banks. A unidirectional gateway is deployed to monitor the equipment-critical network while preventing any online attacks on the protective relays.

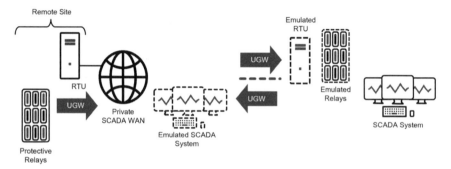

*Figure (24) Unidirectionally-Protected Relays and Central SCADA Site*

## Replicas DMZ

Information transmitted from control-critical to IT networks is frequently very valuable – this value is generally the motive for integrating ICS with IT networks. The IT teams responsible for protecting the information in replica servers and emulated industrial devices often deploy these replicas in a DMZ network, separated from the main IT network with an IT-managed firewall, as part of an IT-SEC system of protecting replicated information.

In this architecture, a unidirectional gateway protects a control-critical network from information/attacks in an IT network, and a DMZ firewall protects the information flowing from the critical network into IT systems.

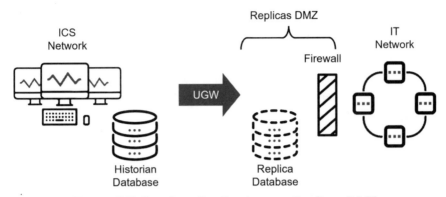

*Figure (25) Database Replication to a Replicas DMZ*

## Wireless Networks

Wireless networks have intrinsic security limitations – the wireless communications medium is inherently broadcast, which permits attackers to both listen to and interfere with wireless communications, without gaining physical access to the industrial site.

Worse, cell phones and a wide variety of other inexpensive, commonplace cyber assets increasingly use wireless communications and sometimes use multiple kinds of wireless communications simultaneously. The ability to use multiple wireless communications mechanisms simultaneously allows cyber attacks to pivot between wireless networks through compromised wireless devices. These characteristics make commonplace devices increasingly convenient as pivot points for wireless attacks on industrial sites for distant attackers. For an example of such pivoting through a cell phone, see attack #10 in Chapter 11.

There are situations when wireless communications are unavoidable, though, such as when physical connectivity with remote stations is not possible. In such cases, SEC-OT sites employ wireless communications and the "SCADA WAN" architecture. Such sites use dedicated/leased wireless frequencies whenever possible, and whenever practical avoid the use of commodity signalling systems such as Wi-Fi and SMS, which are available to even unskilled attackers.

There are also circumstances when wireless communications are very desirable, to reduce capital and operating costs at industrial sites. One reference architecture with minimal risk uses wireless communications to send monitoring data to IT networks or portable devices through a unidirectional gateway.

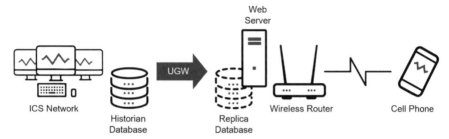

ICS Network    Historian        Replica        Wireless Router        Cell Phone
               Database         Database

*Figure (26) Unidirectional Database Replication to a Wireless Network*

With this design, no compromise of the wireless equipment or portable devices can reach back into the critical network to affect operations. There is, however, still a risk that a sophisticated attack can tamper with the monitoring data that reaches portable devices.

For such attacks to have physical consequences, information from the devices, or in wirelessly-reachable external networks, must return into the control-critical network to miscontrol physical equipment. SEC-OT best practices address this threat. Sites using unidirectionally-protected wireless monitoring are advised to review the "Deceived Insiders" section in Chapter 4.

## Summary

Unidirectional database replication and device emulation are the most commonly used unidirectional reference architectures. The complete list of reference architectures is:

| Database Replication | Device Emulation | Application Replication | Remote Diagnostics and Maintenance |
|---|---|---|---|
| Emergency Maintenance | Continuous Remote Operation | Device Data Sniffing | Central or Cloud SOC |
| Network IDS | Convenient File Transfer | IIoT and Cloud Communications | Electronic Mail and Browsing |
| Partial Replication | Scheduled Updates | Safety Systems | Continuous High-Level Control |
| SCADA WAN | Protective Relays | Replicas DMZ | Wireless Networks |

SEC-OT pioneers continue inventing new reference architectures as they encounter new kinds of industrial networking needs.

# Chapter 7  Power Generation Case Study

This chapter presents an example of the first phase of a transition from a non-SEC-OT to a SEC-OT security program at a pair of electric power plants. This first phase had online protections as a focus.

At each of these two plants, a small DCS network was managed according to an ICS engineering-change-control discipline, with all remaining cyber assets either in an IT network or in an IT/OT DMZ. IT personnel were responsible for the equipment in the DMZ and managed the equipment to IT-SEC standards. Much of this equipment though, was interacting heavily with the DCS. Some of the equipment was dual-homed, with connections both to the IT-managed DMZ as well as to the DCS network or to control devices directly. Some of the equipment routinely issued control commands to those control devices. DCS hosts and control devices ran no antivirus system, were not part of any Windows domain and applied security updates only when the DCS software was upgraded, roughly every five years.

Some time before the SEC-OT implementation, plant personnel had started taking on increased responsibility for ICS security and had installed an ICS-managed firewall between the IT firewall and the IT DMZ. The rationale for this firewall was that ICS personnel should be responsible for which cyber assets and which people were permitted access to control-critical resources in the DMZ. This complicated IT management of the DMZ however, since every new or changed connection into the DMZ needed by IT teams required a change request to, and approval and implementation by, the ICS team.

In addition, a network IDS monitored the DCS network and reported to a corporate SOC, the local grid control center had connections through firewalls to DNP3 revenue meters measuring high-voltage power flows into the grid and this grid control center also had a DNP3 connection that instructed the DCS as to how much power to produce, second by second.

A smaller version of the same architecture existed at a smaller natural-gas-fired plant located nearby. The smaller site had a local operator only 8x5. Off hours, weekends and most holidays, the operator at the main plant was responsible for operating the smaller site by remote control. The remote-control connection was tunnelled through the IT network to the smaller site using a network VPN capability built into the OT firewall.

The result of a preliminary survey of equipment, connectivity and information flows is summarized in the figure below:

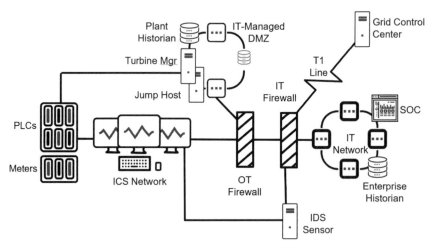

*Figure (27) Original Main Site Network*

Many of these components were deployed in either dual redundant or hot-standby redundant configurations. To simplify the diagram above and related discussions, this chapter ignores redundant equipment and data paths and discusses the system as if there were only one instance of each kind of equipment.

Noteworthy components in each network include:

- An IDS gathering data from mirror ports and publishing alerts to the IT network,

- A private communications path from the grid control center to the IT firewall,

- Production meters reporting current production to both the control center and the DCS,

- Phasor Measurement Units (PMUs) measuring the phase angle of all three phases of power connected to the grid and reporting those measurements through the IT network and Internet to university researchers in another state (not illustrated),

- A turbine management and maintenance system in the DMZ,

- A jump host in the DMZ providing remote access to IT and turbine vendor personnel, and

- Plant historian servers in each site's DMZ, with an enterprise historian in another city. Both plant historians were aggregated into the enterprise historian with a software database synchronization tool.

## Defining the Critical WAN

A preliminary SEC-OT classification effort identified:

- **Production meters at the primary site:** Control-critical, because those meters provided production feedback to the main-site DCS. Production meters at the smaller site were not used by that site's DCS, only by power grid accounting systems. These smaller-site meters were classified as IT equipment because their failure had only business consequences in the form of billing anomalies.

- **Each DCS:** Control-critical.

- **All assets in the IT-managed DMZ networks:** Control-critical, except for the remote access jump hosts.

- **Jump hosts, IDS sensors and PMUs:** IT-centric, because none of this equipment is involved in real-time control of either the main or secondary site.

A new ICS network was proposed for each site, connecting the DCS network to new servers proposed for the site. To reclassify IT-managed DMZ equipment as control-critical equipment, new Active Directory and antivirus servers were proposed for both sites' new ICS networks, and all DMZ hosts, except the jump hosts, were proposed to be converted to use these new infrastructure servers instead of the IT-network equivalents.

To facilitate continuous remote operation from the main site to the smaller site for off-hours operation, the SEC-OT team proposed purchasing a private, leased connection between the sites. Both the main site and smaller site's new ICS networks and existing DCS networks were grouped into a single control-critical WAN.

Unidirectional gateways were proposed to protect the critical WAN from information/attack flows from both the grid control center and the IT network. The gateways were oriented outbound-only from the small site ICS network, and both inbound and outbound at the main site. An emergency access unit was proposed between the jump host and the ICS firewall at the main site only. The proposed SEC-OT main site network is illustrated below:

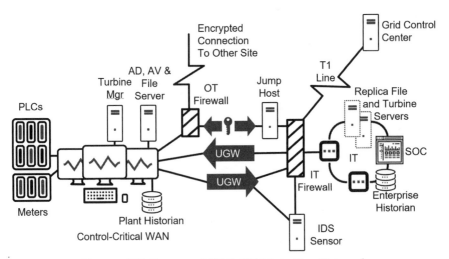

*Figure (28) Proposed SEC-OT Main Site Network*

## Unidirectional Architectures

This initial SEC-OT proposal used a number of unidirectional network reference architectures:

### *Overall:*

- **Continuous Remote Operation:** Leased, dedicated communications capacity was proposed to connect the main plant to the smaller plant, and both sites together were proposed to be managed and protected as a single control-critical network. A set of OT firewalls established an encrypted, site-to-site VPN between the main plant and the smaller plant.

### *Main Site Outbound To IT:*

- **Database Replication:** Several databases were proposed to be replicated:

  - The DCS historian databases were proposed to be replicated from each site to the IT network, aggregating all historian content into the enterprise historian database. Both databases were to be replicated via the outbound unidirectional gateway at the main site.

  - All turbine management databases were proposed to be replicated to the IT network for the turbine vendor to access via an IT VPN connection.

- **Emergency Maintenance:** An emergency access device was proposed to enable vendor management of the turbine control systems. The vendor was proposed to connect to the IT-managed jump host across a VPN and request the site to activate the emergency access device. This one mechanism was proposed to provide access to control-critical equipment at both sites via the leased connection between the sites.

- **Network Intrusion Detection Systems:** The SEC-OT team proposed to mirror port traffic captures from the ICS and DCS networks to the IT-managed IDS sensor.

- **Device Emulation:** The emulation of production meters was proposed, emulating meters from both the main site and smaller site to the IT firewall, for use by the grid control center.

- **Central or Cloud SOC:** The emulation of Syslog and SNMP clients was proposed from control-critical equipment at both sites to a corporate SOC.

- **Server Replication:** The replication of a file server at the main site to the IT network was proposed. This server would be available for use by personnel with access to critical network equipment at both sites for ad-hoc file transfers to reduce the use of USB drives.

### Main Site Inbound from IT:

- **Device Emulation:** The emulation of the grid control center DNP3 master device to the main site's DCS was proposed to provide the DCS with power production setpoints.

- **Scheduled Updates:** The inbound unidirectional gateway was proposed to pull antivirus signatures periodically and supply them to the new ICS AV server at the main site.

### Small Site Outbound (not illustrated):

- **Network Intrusion Detection Systems:** Mirror port traffic captures were proposed to be replicated from the ICS network to the IT-managed IDS sensor. Unlike other replications from the small site that were routed through the private communications link to the main site, mirror port traffic represented too high a volume of traffic to send through that link. Instead, a unidirectional gateway was proposed for the smaller site for the sole purpose of replicating high volumes of network traffic captures to the IDS sensor at that site.

A subsequent detailed analysis of existing data flows and the proposed solution revealed that the enterprise relied on a small number of historian database experts at a central site who managed both the enterprise historian

81

and all the plant historians, excepting only the turbine historians. Turbine historians were managed by the turbine vendors.

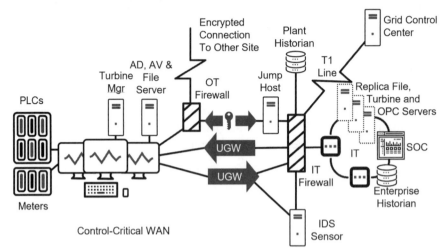

*Figure (29) As-Built SEC-OT Main Site Network*

Rather than establish a private communications infrastructure and deploy the Continuous Remote Operation reference architecture for these central experts, the team decided to reclassify the two plants' DCS historians as IT assets, consolidate the two into a single historian on the IT network at the main plant, and use the Device Emulation architecture to replicate DCS OPC-DA servers to the IT network rather than replicating the historians.

In the new network architecture, plant personnel manage all control-critical cyber assets using the engineering-change-control discipline and IT personnel manage all IT assets. The access unit gives site personnel physical control over remote access to the critical network. The new division of responsibility though, means that such remote access is needed much less frequently than was the case when IT personnel were managing control equipment in the original DMZ.

## Summary

Improved protection from online attacks was the focus of a SEC-OT upgrade at a pair of power plants. An operator at the larger plant frequently operated the smaller facility remotely. The original design of the network had confused IT and ICS responsibilities, with IT personnel managing certain control-critical assets to IT-SEC standards rather than to ICS engineering-change-controlled standards.

The SEC-OT upgrade moved all control-critical equipment into the ICS network, and modelled IDS sensors, the jump host and both plant historian servers as IT assets. None of the IT assets were involved in continuous, control-critical operations.

A private connection between sites was purchased using dedicated telecommunications facilities. The sum of all ICS, DCS and related networking equipment at both sites was grouped together as a single control-critical WAN.

A unidirectional gateway was deployed at the main site to replicate:

- OPC servers from both plants' DCS networks to the main-plant IT network for use by the main-plant historian,

- Main-plant network mirror ports to an IT IDS sensor,

- Control-critical Syslog and SNMP security clients at both plants to the IT network for use by enterprise SOC,

- Revenue meters to the IT network for use by the power grid control center, and

- A new file server to the IT network to eliminate routine USB drive usage.

An inbound unidirectional gateway was deployed to update the ICS AV server periodically with new AV signatures and replicate the grid control center to the DCS so that the DCS could poll the replica for new power production setpoints.

All ICS equipment at both plants was configured to trust a new ICS Active Directory and antivirus server. In the new network design, all control-critical equipment is managed by ICS personnel, according to ICS engineering-change-control and SEC-OT principles.

# Chapter 8  Security Monitoring

Security monitoring, incident response and incident recovery were identified in Chapter 1 as essential parts of a comprehensive security program. This chapter describes how security monitoring is particularly significant to SEC-OT security programs.

## Monitoring Basics

Intrusion detection systems (IDS) and Security Information and Event Management (SIEM) systems are the foundation of security monitoring. IDS include network-based and host-based systems that monitor for symptoms of attacks and raise alerts when such symptoms are detected. Security monitoring is the process of gathering a wide array of IDS and other security, network, host and application information and alerts into a SIEM for display, analysis and correlation to support security posture assessment, security problem diagnosis and incident response.

Intrusion detection and security monitoring are detective, not preventive, measures. Security monitoring cannot reliably prevent the compromise of industrial systems but can sometimes limit the consequences of compromise, when compromise and attacks in progress are detected early enough to remediate before physical consequences are incurred.

Security monitoring of ICS networks, while not reliably detecting or preventing compromise, does tend to detect attacks, compromise and other anomalies more reliably than such monitoring of IT networks. The ICS engineering-change-control discipline produces ICS networks that change very slowly. This means that IDS and security monitoring systems can be tuned very precisely as to the kinds of communications and host activity that are normal for an ICS network, and so can produce alarms more reliably for activity that is not normal.

> **Note**
>
> *More important than incident response, industrial enterprises can optimize only what they measure. Security monitoring provides important insights into, and measurements of, the status of a security system.*

## Near-Miss Programs

At SEC-OT sites, security monitoring and incident response are also the foundation of cyber-near-miss programs. Removable media near-miss programs need instrumentation of cyber assets to report attempts to mount

85

removable media. Removable device programs need instrumentation of both cyber assets and network components to report connections of unauthorized devices. Security monitoring can also include the instrumentation of removable devices themselves to record when those devices have been put at risk of compromise by a connection to a noncritical asset or network.

Continuous monitoring and prompt response to near-miss alerts for removable media and devices provide valuable, real-time feedback to ICS technicians and vendors who are making mistakes with such media and devices.

## IT-SEC Costs and Risks

In IT-SEC programs for ICS networks, security monitoring can raise concerns about introducing a new single point of compromise. All communications paths through firewalls that permit security monitoring data to flow to a central monitoring station also permit attacks to flow back into the monitored industrial networks.

Some experts also express a concern that most IT SOC analysts have no experience with or understanding of ICS networks and applications. The concern is that such analysts are unable to monitor ICS networks effectively, and without human monitoring, follow-up actions and investigations, security monitoring technology has little value. This concern is misplaced. IT SOC analysts typically have neither ICS training nor experience because they have no need for such experience, nor opportunity to apply such knowledge if they do have it.

It is only when central SOCs are about to be connected to monitor ICS networks that ICS training for SOC analysts has benefit. Once SOC analysts are trained and start to work with ICS security data, they quickly develop the expertise that industrial enterprises require in their central SOCs. ICS expertise is a consequence of monitoring ICS networks from a central SOC, not a prerequisite for such monitoring.

## Typical SEC-OT Deployment

SEC-OT sites are generally connected to one or more company-wide SIEMs in a central Security Operations Center (SOC). The central SOC may be on the company's IT network, may be cloud-based, or may be outsourced entirely to an offsite security vendor. SEC-OT sites use the Network Intrusion Detection and Central or Cloud SOC reference architectures to provide the SOC with visibility deep into industrial networks without the risk to those networks posed by traditional IT-SEC firewalled connectivity to the central SOC.

SEC-OT enterprises instrument their reliability and security test beds in much greater detail than they do their production ICS networks. Some sites deploy a secondary SIEM user interface near the engineering workstations used to manage their test beds. The local SIEM user interface allows ICS testing personnel to cooperate more effectively with SOC analysts in analyzing and interpreting security intelligence that is gathered from candidate hardware, software, configurations and other complex information artifacts being tested.

## Summary

Extending IT-SEC connectivity deep into ICS networks in order to monitor those networks introduces as many security risks as such extension remediates. The SEC-OT approach of forwarding security information unidirectionally introduces no such risks. Essentially all SEC-OT sites are connected to a central IT SOC or outsourced cloud SOC via the Central or Cloud SOC and Network Intrusion Detection System reference architectures.

Security monitoring is a vital part of SEC-OT removable media and removable device near-miss programs. More fundamentally, industrial sites can optimize only what they measure. Security monitoring is one way of measuring the strength of security programs in support of continuous improvement of those programs.

# Chapter 9  Deploy Compensating Measures

No security posture is perfect. Defence in depth teaches that when primary SEC-OT physical defences for cyber attacks are somehow breached, secondary IT-SEC defences must be in place to help prevent at least some kinds of compromise and/or reduce the consequences of compromise.

> **Definition**
>
> ***Compensating Measures*** *– secondary software security measures used when primary physical protections against information/attack flows are imperfect or cannot be fully deployed*

Some IT-SEC compensating measures, however, are seen by most ICS practitioners as unduly costly or as introducing greater risk than the measures mitigate. This chapter discusses the most controversial IT-SEC compensating measures and shows how these measures are routinely used within SEC-OT security programs.

## Uncontroversial Measures

SEC-OT sites generally deploy a wide variety of IT-SEC security, software, and procedural defences, in addition to SEC-OT physical defences. Catalogues of such conventional IT-SEC mechanisms can be found in guidance such as the NIST 800-53 Rev 4[6] standard and ISO 27000[7] family of standards. Many IT-SEC techniques are uncontroversial, for example:

- Using "secure" hardware and software components certified to ICS security standards such as ISASecure[8],

- Developing new software components with secure software development processes,

- Using backups to simplify recovery after accidental or deliberately-induced failures, and

---

6   *NIST Special Publication 800-53 Revision 4 – Security and Privacy Controls for Federal Information Systems and Organizations,* National Institute of Standards and Technology, 2013

7   *IEC/ISO 27000 family – Information security management systems,* International Organization for Standardization, 2013

8   *ISASecure – IEC 62443 Conformance Certification,* International Society for Automation

- Disabling or removing unnecessary software and features, to reduce ICS complexity and improve resistance to certain kinds of attack.

Many such defences can be deployed only after a significant engineering review and testing process to ensure that the changes do not pose an unacceptable risk to safe or reliable physical operations. Over time, SEC-OT sites generally carry out such reviews and testing and apply these uncontroversial changes either to existing systems or to new systems as control equipment is upgraded.

---

**Note**

*Practitioners are cautioned that ICS sites still in transition to SEC-OT practices are exposed to routine compromise by many IT-class threats.*

*The SEC-OT exemptions and simplifications below that assume a mature SEC-OT program may not apply to transitional sites.*

---

## Security Updates

Security update programs are a perennial source of controversy and conflict. Security update programs install software changes that ICS and IT software vendors claim will fix certain known software vulnerabilities. In the absence of such fixes, both common malware and custom malware can exploit these vulnerabilities. The simplest of known vulnerabilities can be exploited by any user with access to the ICS software, for example hard-coded passwords and command-line back doors. Applying security updates reduces the amount of software in an ICS that is vulnerable to these attacks.

### Security Update Costs and Risks

Security updates are imperfect. Security updates may introduce new reliability or safety risks, may introduce new vulnerabilities and may fail to correct the very vulnerabilities for which the update was nominally created. In addition, security updates are intrinsically limited in that they do nothing to address zero-day vulnerabilities, exploits of permissions, exploits of system configurations or exploits of stolen passwords and other credentials.

ICS security update programs are frequently very expensive. Every security update is a change to ICS software. ICS vendors rarely supply descriptions of these software changes in enough detail to carry out an effective engineering assessment of the risk of deploying the changed software. While most vendors make a significant effort to test their changed software, no vendor can test the changes in all the different contexts in which the vendors' ICS software is deployed at very different industrial sites. As a result, at most sites there is significant risk that applying security updates will result in ICS failures that trigger site shutdowns or worse.

Nearly all industrial sites, therefore, test security updates as exhaustively as practical before deployment. SEC-OT sites are no exception to this rule. As was indicated in Chapter 4, SEC-OT sites test security updates for security threats as well as for more conventional safety and reliability failures. Testing security updates is very costly, considering how frequently security updates are released by vendors of the largest software applications, such as web browsers, relational databases and operating systems, and considering how thoroughly new software must be tested to be confident of the software's security, reliability and safety characteristics.

### Typical Security Update Programs

All SEC-OT sites have security update programs and the frequency of updates depends on the kind of equipment being updated.

> **Note**
>
> *A truism of IT/OT relations is that:*
>
> *IT people must understand that some OT equipment is special and is not a good candidate for aggressive, IT-style security update and anti-malware programs.*
>
> *OT people in turn must understand that not all OT equipment is special, and that much of it can and should be managed with aggressive, IT-style security update and anti-malware programs.*

For example, remote access jump hosts in the Emergency Maintenance reference architecture are exposed to IT-network threats and so must be managed as IT assets, with frequent security and AV updates. No control-critical network depends on these jump hosts for correct operation. If a faulty security update disables a jump host until the host can be restored from backups, physical operations continue unimpeded. More generally, any asset on a control-critical network that is turned off most of the time, or otherwise not essential to second-by-second operation, can generally be updated more aggressively than more reliability-critical assets.

For critical equipment though, the time needed to thoroughly test updates and the cost of such testing demand that the frequency of security updates at SEC-OT sites is considerably lower than is demanded by IT-SEC standards. Sites that use SEC-OT practices to eliminate practically all incoming information/attack flows typically apply security updates to control-critical equipment every 3-12 months.

At less-thoroughly-secured SEC-OT sites and at ICS sites using only IT-SEC practices, security updates must be more frequent, no matter the cost. Such sites must balance the safety and reliability risks of continuous updates against the security risks of a slower rate of security updates. The desire to simultaneously reduce security update program risks and costs is a strong driver towards deploying comprehensive SEC-OT practices.

One can argue that there are still ways for the most sophisticated attackers to seed malware into a SEC-OT critical network – nothing is secure after all. Arguing that the risk due to the most sophisticated attackers justifies high-risk, high-cost and high-frequency security update programs, though, is incorrect. The most sophisticated attackers can also discover and weaponize their own ICS software zero days and thus defeat software update programs. In practice, low-update-frequency SEC-OT sites are significantly more secure than high-update-frequency IT-SEC sites, as can be seen in Chapters 10-12.

Again, mature SEC-OT sites have security-update programs and apply such programs to all equipment for which updates are practical. For example, air-gapped server room thermostats that can be reprogrammed only by dismantling the device and reflashing the EPROM with a special programmer, might never be updated. Physically distant and unidirectionally-protected RTUs and protective relays might be updated only as often as work crews are physically dispatched to those sites for other reasons. Equipment at central sites might be updated on the 3-12-month test-bed schedule. Noncritical equipment on control-critical networks might be updated more frequently.

## Anti-Malware Systems

Anti-malware systems are controversial as well. Antivirus, application whitelisting and sand-boxing systems are examples of different kinds of anti-malware systems. Each has different features and limitations:

* Signature-based antivirus systems identify malware components that match specific patterns called signatures but tend to be blind to malware that is new, low-volume, custom or memory-based. Sometimes these systems are blind to very old malware as well, whose signatures have been retired.

* Application whitelisting systems permit only executable code that matches a "permitted" list to run. Whitelisting systems tend to be blind

to memory-based and some scripted malware and tend to be vulnerable to certain kinds of forged software and security updates.

- Sand-boxing systems generally run in a cloud environment and open suspect files in a temporary virtual machine, looking for suspicious behaviour. Malware authors work to identify the sandbox environment in their malware and program the malware to remain idle and benign in the sandbox environment. Sand-box vendors in turn work to make the sandbox environment as indistinguishable from a real target as possible.

In practice, the combination of all three anti-malware systems can detect and quarantine most high-volume malware but can be defeated by sophisticated, custom malware. In addition, all anti-malware systems are software and all software has vulnerabilities that may be exploited.

### Anti-Malware Costs and Risks

Signature-based and whitelisting antivirus systems generally recommend running a complete scan of protected computers periodically. Such scans are resource intensive and significantly impair the operation of the computer being scanned. ICS vendors often do not recommend such scans for the most critical ICS equipment.

In addition, signature-based AV systems rely on frequent signature updates. With each such update, there is a risk that the new signature set contains signatures that will trigger false-positive actions – if a new signature accidentally matches legitimate components of the ICS, then the AV system will quarantine and disable those components. It is therefore imperative that new signatures not be deployed directly to the ICS but be deployed on a test bed first, one that contains at least "one of each" kind and version of software deployed anywhere in the ICS. Once a comprehensive AV scan of such a test bed completes without incident using new signatures, the signatures can be deployed on live ICS equipment.

More generally, both AV and application whitelisting systems insert themselves into the software interface between running ICS applications and the operating system kernel. Such insertion dramatically alters ICS execution paths. For this reason, most ICS vendors support a limited number of AV and whitelisting systems – the systems that the vendors have tested extensively. This means that when a given ICS installation uses products from many ICS vendors, the site may need infrastructure in place to support and update multiple anti-malware vendors' products.

Sand-boxing systems are most commonly cloud-based, and so are most suitable to perimeter kiosks and the external side of unidirectional gateways. Sand-boxing is not real time and so is not suitable for deployment on most ICS equipment.

### Typical Anti-Malware Deployment

SEC-OT sites generally deploy anti-malware systems nearly universally throughout their control-critical networks. Up-to-date anti-malware protections are especially important for removable media kiosks, heavily-instrumented test beds and any equipment where removable media, USB drives and other removable devices cannot be both physically and logically disabled. This widespread deployment of anti-malware products at mature SEC-OT sites is despite the fact that such sites have already eliminated practically all opportunity for common malware to enter control-critical networks.

Mature SEC-OT sites make only a small number of practical exceptions to an "AV everywhere" policy, exceptions such as:

* Exempting some air-gapped equipment,

* Exempting equipment whose operating systems have no anti-malware products available, for example some kinds of protective relays and SIS controllers, and

* Reluctantly exempting equipment that is essential to real-time ICS operations and whose vendors do not yet support anti-malware protections of any sort.

Anti-malware systems are a useful second level of protection against high-volume, unsophisticated malware and SEC-OT sites generally deploy such protection as widely as is practical.

## Encryption and Cryptographic Authentication

Encryption and authentication systems are used routinely at high levels of abstraction in industrial control systems, but other uses are more controversial. The following discussion explores highlights of the ICS encryption debate.

In principle, encryption and cryptographic authentication make intercepted communications unreadable and make legitimate communications unforgeable, for any attacker who does not have access to the necessary cryptographic keys. In practice though:

* All cryptosystems are software and all software has both known and unknown vulnerabilities,

- Operating systems and other platform software essential to cryptosystems may be compromisable by unencrypted attacks at lower levels of abstraction than the cryptosystem,

- Attackers who gain access to cryptographic keys can compromise cryptosystems comparatively easily, and

- Legitimate endpoints of encrypted communications always have routine access to the means to encrypt and decrypt their communications. Such endpoints can therefore be used to attack each other, or pivot attacks into each other, via encrypted communications.

Despite these limitations, encryption has benefits for ICS networks. In the absence of encryption and authentication, attackers or malware with a foothold in a critical network can simply connect to control devices such as PLCs and RTUs and issue whatever commands the attacker wishes to these devices. With no robust way to distinguish legitimate from forged communications, control endpoints simply execute the commands that attackers send them.

This problem is especially acute in SCADA and other applications where control commands must traverse a WAN to reach the control endpoints. Even when the WAN is a private network, physically tampering with elements of the WAN that are located outside of a site's physical security perimeter generally permits attackers to inject forged content into ICS communications. When WAN communications are encrypted and authenticated, it is more difficult for such attackers to use forged communications to impair physical operations.

### Encryption Costs and Risks

Universal encryption of ICS communications has been a controversial topic for over a decade. The benefits of encryption seem clear, but ICS practitioners argue that:

- Training is an issue – many sites struggle to teach technicians replacing equipment what an IP address is, much less what a cryptographic key is and how to manage and manipulate such keys during emergency equipment replacements.

- Different types of encryption and cryptographic authentication can consume significant CPU resources, thus reducing the throughput and responsiveness of critical systems.

- Unencrypted communications behind many layers of physical and software protections represent minimal risk. Good ICS security programs should make it practically impossible for attackers or their malware to reach deep enough into an ICS network to reach nonencrypting devices.

- Key management for hundreds or thousands of ICS devices at an industrial site is difficult and poorly automated, and key expiry is a threat to continuous and reliable operations.

- Encryption makes packet sniffing and some other kinds of emergency debugging difficult or impossible, impairing security, safety and reliability emergency responses.

### Typical Deployments
SEC-OT sites always deploy encryption for communications traversing a WAN and sometimes deploy multiple layers of encryption for such traversals. Mature SEC-OT sites also activate encryption on all equipment where such activation is practical, including essentially all communications with high-level applications such as plant historians and file servers. Since at mature SEC-OT sites, it is practically impossible for malware, vendors or other attackers to gain access to protected control-critical networks, such sites are generally willing to make a small number of practical exceptions to a "strong encryption everywhere" policy, including:

- Relaxing IT-SEC rules for key expiry for the most critical systems, so that key updating errors and omissions do not introduce new risks to continuous operations, and

- Reluctantly exempting equipment that does not yet support encryption, when such equipment is otherwise protected by mature and robust SEC-OT programs.

The latter exemption is unfortunately very common at present, since the most older ICS control and monitoring devices do not support the encryption features built into modern devices. Mature SEC-OT sites make encryption, role-based authentication and other standard IT-SEC features mandatory when purchasing new ICS equipment.

The issue of gaining access to encrypted communications for debugging is one that has only vendor-specific solutions at present, not general ones.

## Summary
In practice, SEC-OT sites apply IT-SEC practices extensively, as compensating measures to complement the primary, physical protections against information/attack flows required by SEC-OT principles and practices.

A small number of IT-SEC practices are controversial in ICS networks. SEC-OT sites resolve these controversies as follows. Essentially all SEC-OT sites:

• Maintain nearly-universal security-update programs whose update frequency reflects the criticality of equipment to ICS operations and the exposure of such equipment to cyber attacks,

• Maintain nearly-universal anti-malware programs, and

• Deploy encryption universally for WAN communications and as universally as vendor support permits for ICS LANs.

Sites in transition to SEC-OT must deploy IT-SEC protections more aggressively and comprehensively than mature SEC-OT sites, in a difficult balance between IT-style costs and risks versus ICS safety and reliability imperatives. Mature SEC-OT sites make very few exemptions to IT-SEC programs but do so confidently due to the strength of SEC-OT physical protections against offline and online information/attack flows.

# Chapter 10   Assess Residual Risks

Every enterprise, and sometimes every site, has different tolerances for risk. High-tech start-ups for example generally take much greater risks than do established businesses. Assessing and managing residual cyber risk is therefore an important function at industrial sites. Since nothing is secure, there is always residual risk. The question "is this site secure?" is meaningless – security is a continuum, not a binary state. The question "how secure is this site?" is more useful. The question "how secure should this site be?" is even more useful. This chapter introduces the SEC-OT approach to capabilities-based assessments of residual risks due to cyber attacks.

The risks that are the focus of SEC-OT capabilities-based assessments are risks with physical consequences for industrial processes, including:

* Unplanned production shutdowns,

* Impaired production quantities or qualities,

* Damage to physical equipment,

* Casualties at the industrial site,

* Public safety threats, and

* Environmental disasters.

SEC-OT sites and enterprises consider physical consequences of widely-available attack capabilities when assessing how secure a given site is, or should be. IT-SEC risk assessments, in contrast, tend to give more weight to software vulnerabilities and estimates of attacker motivations than to attack capabilities. Vulnerabilities and motives can change very quickly though, invalidating the conclusions of IT-SEC risk assessments.

Risk assessments for SEC-OT sites measure well-understood attack capabilities against the capabilities of defensive postures, asking the question "which attacks does this security posture defeat reliably?" A comprehensive assessment often evaluates a very large inventory of possible cyber attacks. Attack capabilities evolve much more slowly than do vulnerabilities and motives. A risk assessment based on slow-changing criteria yields conclusions about cyber risk that change only very slowly.

## Design Basis Threat

SEC-OT borrows the term Design Basis Threat (DBT) from the physical security discipline:

> **Definition**
>
> **Design Basis Threat (DBT)** – *the set of attacks a site is designed to defeat reliably*

In the physical security domain for example, a certain government site might be required to defeat reliably a small group of terrorists who are trained and armed in a certain way, but not an assault by an enemy army, supported by tanks and fighter jets.

In the cyber domain, DBT is a useful tool for communicating risk to business decision makers. Nothing is secure, so there is always a set of attacks that a given cybersecurity posture does not defeat reliably. Cyber DBT can be illustrated as a line drawn through a list of representative attacks, separating the cyber attacks a site defeats reliably from those not so defeated. In the set of attacks not defeated reliably, there are always some attacks that are easier to carry out than others.

It is the cheapest and simplest attacks above the DBT line that define the DBT line in the minds of business decision makers. By describing these simplest cyber attacks not defeated reliably, it is possible to engage these decision-makers in useful dialog as to whether the DBT line should be moved higher or lower.

## Reliably Defeating Attacks

To defeat an attack reliably means to prevent the physical consequence of the attack essentially every time this class of attack is launched. For example:

* **Antivirus systems** – do not defeat common malware reliably, because malware attacks are launched into the wild before antivirus signatures are available for the attacks. If common malware reaches a vulnerable system between the time the malware was launched and the time that AV signatures are available and applied, the targeted system is most likely compromised, despite the deployed AV system.

* **Security updates** – do not defeat exploits of known vulnerabilities reliably. For example, when an operating system vendor issues a security update, it takes time for the control system vendor to verify that this update is, to the ICS vendor's best understanding, compatible with

the vendor's ICS product. It takes additional time for a specific site to test the update on their test bed and determine that the update appears to introduce no new and unacceptable threats to safe and continuous operation. ICS networks are vulnerable to exploits of the known vulnerability during this time interval, despite the existence of a security update program. In addition, security updates are occasionally erroneous, and when erroneous, are not effective in eliminating the known vulnerability that is their motivation.

- **Intrusion detection systems and security monitoring systems** – are detective, not preventive measures. As important as IDS and security monitoring are to near miss programs as well as ongoing maintenance and optimization of security programs, these measures do not defeat attacks reliably. Intrusion detection and incident response take time. In that time, compromised ICS components and physical equipment may be operated either manually by a remote attacker, or automatically by autonomous malware, which may be enough to bring about the physical consequences the site's security program seeks to prevent.

In contrast, the following are examples of security measures that do defeat a specific class of attack reliably:

- **Remote, password-theft, phishing attacks** – two-factor authentication based on RSA-style password dongles reliably defeats password phishing attempts. One could postulate an attack that physically steals the password dongle, but that would no longer be a "phishing" attack. A remote attacker who can forge email and produce look-alike websites, but cannot steal physical items locally, is not able to defeat this type of two-factor protection system.

- **Encryption key scraping software** – trusted platform modules (TPMs) reliably defeat attempts to search compromised computers' memory and persistent storage to steal encryption keys. TPM hardware is designed so that encryption keys never leave the dedicated, cryptographic hardware modules, nor appear in memory in the computer running the TPM. More sophisticated attacks, such as physically dismantling the hardware modules of stolen computers, might succeed in retrieving these encryption keys. Such attacks though, are no longer the indicated attack – software searching a machine's memory and hard drive for keys.

- **Internet-controlled malware** – unidirectional gateways reliably defeat Internet-controlled malware. The gateways are physically able to send information in only one direction – from a control-critical network to an IT/corporate/Internet network, with no ability to send information back.

In unidirectionally-protected networks, no control signal is physically able to be sent from the Internet to malware on a compromised ICS network.

In short, "defeats reliably" is a high standard. Achieving this standard is generally possible only by describing an attack and a target's defences very specifically.

## Summary

A design-basis threat (DBT) specification describes the most capable cyber attack that an ICS site is required to defeat reliably. "Defeat reliably" is a high standard. Signature-based antivirus systems, for example, do not defeat common malware reliably, because it takes time to create and propagate signatures. In another example, security update programs do not defeat such malware reliably either, because it takes time to test and validate updates, time during which the malware might strike a nonupdated ICS network.

Since nothing is secure, there are always attacks that will breach any given IT-SEC, SEC-OT or other security posture. The question is: how much effort does an attacker need to invest to succeed in their attack? The simplest attacks not defeated reliably are the attacks that business decision-makers need to understand most, to determine whether the DBT line should be raised or lowered in the spectrum of known attack capabilities.

# Chapter 11  The Top 20 ICS Cyber Attacks

This chapter proposes a standard list of 20 cyber attacks to consider when evaluating a defensive design. The list can be useful to sites new to capabilities-based risk assessments. The list can also serve as a standard, representative set of attacks to use when comparing the strength of security postures between sites and between enterprises. This chapter presents the list of attacks while Chapter 12 evaluates the list of attacks against pre-SEC-OT and SEC-OT security design examples.

Each attack in the list indicates both the level of sophistication of the attack and attackers, and the consequences of the attack:

*Sophistication* is a characteristic of both the attack, and the attacker. Sophistication considers questions such as: Did the attack use standard attack tools downloaded from the Internet, professional-grade tools, or custom-built tools? Are the attackers cyber experts? Do they need to understand the physics of the industrial process, to bring about their attack goals? Do they need to understand the design of relevant industrial control systems enough to connect physical outcomes with cyber manipulations? How much inside information that is not available from public sources do the attackers need in order to design and carry out their attack? Do the attackers have inside assistance? Or can they execute the entire attack from outside of their target organizations?

*Consequences* include physical states of the industrial system that a site seeks to avoid and changes in control system computers that need to be restored to their original state, even if those changes have not yet resulted in measurable effects on the physical process. Physical consequences are most often one of: impaired or poor-quality production, unexpected shutdown of a physical production process, damage to physical equipment, casualties at the site, environmental disasters and threats to public safety.

The list of 20 attacks is presented in a generally least-sophisticated to most-sophisticated order. Exceptions to this rule occur so that sets of related attacks can be grouped together.

## #1 ICS Insider

A disgruntled control-system technician steals passwords by "shoulder surfing" other technicians, logs in to equipment controlling the physical process using the stolen passwords and issues shutdown instructions to parts of the physical process, thus triggering a partial plant shutdown.

*Sophistication:* This is a moderately sophisticated attack. ICS technicians tend to have a good knowledge of how to operate control system components to bring about specific goals, such as a shutdown, but less knowledge of fundamental engineering concepts or safety systems that are designed into industrial processes.

*Consequences:* This class of incident is most often able to cause a partial or complete plant shutdown. More serious physical consequences may be possible, depending on the insider and on details of the industrial process.

## #2 IT Insider

A disgruntled IT insider "shoulder-surfs" remote access credentials entered by an ICS support technician who is visiting a remote office. The disgruntled insider later uses the credentials to log into the same distant ICS engineering workstation that the technician logged into. The insider looks around the workstation and eventually finds and starts a development copy of the plant HMI. The insider brings up screens at random and presses whatever buttons seem likely to cause the most damage or confusion. These actions trigger a partial plant shutdown.

*Sophistication:* This is an unsophisticated attack. IT insiders generally have little knowledge of cyber systems, control systems or physical processes but often do have social engineering opportunities that can yield credentials able to log into control system networks.

*Consequences:* This class of incident might cause a shutdown or might just cause confusion. At minimum, each such incident triggers an engineering review of settings at the plant, to ensure that no physical equipment has been left misconfigured and able to cause a malfunction in the future.

## #3 Common Ransomware

An engineer searching for technical information from an ICS-connected engineering workstation accidentally downloads ransomware. The malware exploits known vulnerabilities that have not yet been patched on the industrial network, encrypts the engineering workstation, and spreads to most Windows hosts in the ICS. Most Windows hosts in the industrial network are thus encrypted by the attack, shutting down the control system. The impaired control system is unable to bring about an orderly shutdown. Within a few minutes, the plant operator triggers an emergency safety shutdown.

*Variation:* Ransomware infects an IT workstation and spreads via AUTORUN files on network shares, USB drives, and known network vulnerabilities. The ransomware spreads for several days before triggering the encryption process. Multiple machines on both IT and ICS networks are thus infected, with the same consequences as above.

*Sophistication:* Authors of autonomous ransomware can be very sophisticated cyber-wise, producing malware that can spread quickly and automatically through a network while evading common antivirus systems and other security measures. Such authors though, tend to have no understanding of physical industrial processes or industrial control systems.

*Consequences:* Most often, the minimum damage caused by this kind of incident is an unplanned shutdown lasting for as many days as it takes to restore the control system from backups and restart the industrial process – typically 5-10 days of lost production. In the worst case, important equipment can be irreparably damaged by an uncontrolled shutdown. In this case, replacements for the damaged equipment need to be purchased and installed. Where replacements are not readily available, these replacements must be manufactured first, before they can be installed and activated. Worst-case plant downtime in these latter cases can be up to 12 months.

## #4 Targeted Ransomware

An attacker with good computer knowledge targets IT insiders with phishing attacks and malicious attachments, gaining a foothold on the IT network with Remote Access Tool (RAT) malware. The attacker uses the RAT to steal additional credentials, eventually gaining remote access to an industrial control system. The attacker seeds ransomware throughout the ICS and demands a ransom. The site quickly disables all electronic connections between the affected plant and outside networks and tries to pay the ransom. The payment mechanism fails, and the ransomware automatically activates, having received no signal from the attacker that the ransom was paid. The ransomware erases hard drives and BIOS firmware in all infected equipment. The plant suffers an emergency shutdown.

*Sophistication:* The attacker is cyber-sophisticated. Increasingly, organized crime organizations are involved with ransomware. These organizations have access to professional-grade malware toolkits, developers, and RAT operators.

*Consequences:* Computer, network and other equipment with erased firmware generally must be replaced – the equipment has been "bricked" in the parlance of cyber attacks. Again, an emergency shutdown may damage physical equipment, delaying start-up for months.

## #5 Zero-Day Ransomware

An intelligence agency mistakenly leaves a list of zero-day vulnerabilities in operating systems, applications, and firewall sandboxes on an Internet-based command and control center. An attack group, similar to the "Shadow Brokers" who discovered the US National Security Agency (NSA) zero-days, discovers the list and sells it to an organized crime group. This latter group creates autonomous ransomware that propagates by exploiting the zero-day vulnerabilities in file sharing software in the Windows operating system. The malware is released simultaneously on dozens of compromised websites world-wide, and immediately starts to spread. At industrial sites able to share files directly or indirectly with IT networks, the malware jumps through firewalls via encrypted connections to file shares. The compromised file shares infect and encrypt the industrial site, causing an emergency shutdown and damaging physical equipment.

*Sophistication:* Nation-state intelligence agencies are very sophisticated cyber-wise, though generally focused on stealing information rather than causing physical damage. Such agencies routinely discover and/or purchase zero-day vulnerabilities. These agencies have also been known to leak into the public domain some zero days the agencies have discovered or purchased. This attack is very sophisticated cyber-wise but unsophisticated engineering-wise.

*Consequences:* Again, the minimum damage caused by this kind of incident is an unplanned shutdown lasting for as many days as it takes to restore the control system from backups and restart the industrial process – typically 5-10 days of lost production. In the worst case though, important equipment can be irreparably damaged, necessitating costly replacement which make take additional weeks or months.

## #6 Ukrainian Attack

A large group of hacktivist-class attackers steal IT remote-access passwords through phishing attacks. These attackers eventually compromise the IT Windows Domain Controller, create new accounts for themselves, and give the new accounts universal administrative privileges, including access to ICS equipment. The attackers log into the ICS equipment and observe the operation of the ICS HMI until they learn what many of the screens and controls do. When the group attacks, the attackers take control of the HMI and use it to misoperate the physical process. At the same time, co-attackers use their administrative credentials to log into ICS equipment, erase the hard drives, and where practical, erase the equipment firmware.

*Variation:* When targeting other kinds of industries, similar attacks are possible, erasing control system equipment and triggering unplanned shutdowns.

*Sophistication:* The attackers here had good knowledge of cyber systems but limited knowledge of electric distribution processes and control systems.

*Consequences:* The Ukrainian attack is reported to have turned off electric power to nearly one quarter million people for up to 8 hours and erased control system equipment at thirty electric substations. Power was only restored when technicians travelled to each of the affected substations, disconnected control system computers and manually/physically turned on power flows again. More generally, unplanned shutdowns are a consequence of this class of attack, and possibly emergency, uncontrolled shutdowns with the potential for equipment damage that accompanies such shutdowns.

## #7 Sophisticated Ukrainian Attack

A group of attackers is more sophisticated with respect to cyber-attack tools and the engineering details of electric systems. The attack group phishes a low-volume remote access trojan (RAT) into the IT network, such as the BlackEnergy trojan that was reportedly found on IT networks of the utilities impacted by the Ukrainian attack but was not implicated in the attack.

With the RAT, the attackers search for and find additional credentials, eventually compromising the enterprise domain controller. The attack group creates credentials for themselves and logs into ICS servers, reseeding their RAT on the ICS network and ultimately taking over equipment on the ICS network.

Once inside the ICS network, the attack group connects to protective relays and reconfigures them, effectively disabling the relays. The group now sends control commands to very quickly connect and disconnect power flows to parts of the grid, damaging large rotating equipment such as the pumps used by water distribution systems. The attackers also redirect power flows in the small number of high-voltage transmission substations managed by the distribution utilities, destroying high-voltage transformers by overloading and overheating them.

*Sophistication:* This group of attackers is moderately sophisticated, both cyber-wise and engineering-wise.

*Consequences:* Consequences of this attack are more serious. Large water pumps in water distribution systems are damaged, producing drinking water shortages in the affected cities. High voltage transformers must be replaced on an emergency basis, which can take over a week. There is no world-wide inventory of large, high-voltage transformers – while permanent replacements are manufactured, emergency replacements are moved into place from unaffected substations, thus reducing redundancy and capacity in other parts of the electric grid.

## #8 Market Manipulation

An organized crime syndicate targets known vulnerabilities in Internet-exposed services and gains a foothold on IT networks. They seed RAT tools into the compromised system, eventually gaining Windows Domain Admin privileges. The attackers reach into ICS computers that trust the IT Windows domain and propagate RAT technology to those computers. Because the ICS computers are unable to route traffic to the Internet, the attackers route the traffic via peer-to-peer connections using compromised IT equipment.

Once in the ICS network, attackers download and analyze control system configuration files. They then reprogram a single PLC, causing it to misoperate a vital piece of physical equipment, while reporting to the plant HMI that the equipment is operating normally. The equipment wears out prematurely in a season of high demand for the plant's commodity output. The plant shuts down for emergency repair of this apparently random equipment failure.

The same attack occurs at two nearby plants. Once the equipment has failed, the perpetrators erase all evidence of their presence from the affected plants' ICS networks. Prices of the commodity produced at the affected plants spike on commodities markets. When plant production at all plants returns to normal, commodity prices return to normal.

Before and after the attack, the attackers routinely speculate on futures markets for the affected commodity. That these attackers make large profits when commodity prices spike unexpectedly is seen by any potential investigators as normal and legal. The attack is repeated in the next season of high demand.

*Sophistication:* The cyber sophistication of this attack and these attackers is moderate – no zero-days were used, and no code was written. The engineering sophistication of this attack is high. The attackers needed access to an engineer able to interpret the control system configurations, select physical equipment to target, identify the PLC controlling the targeted equipment, download the existing program of the targeted PLC, and design and upload a new program able to wear out the targeted physical equipment prematurely, all while reporting to the HMI that the equipment is operating normally.

*Consequences:* Lost plant production and emergency equipment repair costs.

## #9 Sophisticated Market Manipulation

Sophisticated attackers carry out the market manipulation attack but in a way that is more difficult to defeat. They use known vulnerabilities in Internet-facing systems to compromise the IT network of a services company known to supply services to their real target. The attackers write their own RAT malware and deploy it only at the services company, so that antivirus tools at the services company cannot detect the RAT. The attackers use the RAT to compromise the laptops of personnel who routinely visit the real target. When the attackers detect that the compromised laptops are connected to the real target's IT network, the attackers operate the RAT by remote control and propagate the RAT into the target's IT network.

Inside the target's IT network, the attackers continue to operate the RAT. Intrusion detection systems are blind to the activity of the RAT, because the attack is low-volume, using command lines rather than remote-desktop-style communications. The RAT's command-and-control communications are steganographically-encoded in benign-seeming communications with compromised websites. The attack ultimately propagates to the ICS network, with the same consequences as the Market Manipulation attack.

*Sophistication:* The cyber sophistication of these attackers is high. No zero-days were used, but the attackers developed custom malware with steganographically-encoded communications. The engineering sophistication, like the Market Manipulation attack, is also high.

*Consequences:* Lost plant production for days or weeks and emergency equipment repair costs.

## #10 Cell-phone Wi-Fi

Sophisticated attackers seek to inflict damage on a geography they are unhappy with for some reason. The attackers create a useful, attractive, free cell phone app. The attackers use targeted social media attacks to persuade office workers at critical infrastructure sites in the offending geography to download the free app.

The app runs continuously in the background of the cell phone. While at their critical-infrastructure workplaces, the app instructs the phone to periodically scan for Wi-Fi networks and report such networks to a command and control center. The attackers again, use social media, social engineering and phishing attacks to impersonate insiders at their target organizations, and extract passwords for the Wi-Fi networks. Several of these password-protected networks are part of critical-infrastructure industrial control systems.

The attackers log into these networks using the compromised cell phones and carry out reconnaissance by remote control until they find computer components vulnerable to simple denial of service attacks, such as erasing hard drives or SYN floods. The attackers compromise plant operations, triggering an unplanned shutdown. They then disconnect from the Wi-Fi networks, and then repeat this attack periodically.

*Variation:* Instead of a cell-phone app, attackers use phishing attacks to seed malware on to the desktop computers of office workers who work at the targeted industrial sites, within physical range of ICS Wi-Fi networks.

*Sophistication:* This attack currently needs a high degree of cyber sophistication, because toolkits enabling this type of hidden Wi-Fi hacking from cell phones currently do not exist on the open Internet. Any attackers currently wishing to use this technique would need to write this malware themselves or purchase it from illicit sources. Once such attack tools are widely and publicly available though, this class of attack will come within the means of any hacktivist group with an imagined grievance with industrial enterprises. The attack needs only very low engineering sophistication.

*Consequences:* Repeated plant shutdowns from a source that is difficult to identify. Plant personnel will presumably, eventually determine that the source of the attack is a Wi-Fi network and will shut down all Wi-Fi at the plant, or at least change all the passwords

## #11 Hijacked Two-Factor

Sophisticated attackers seek to compromise operations at an industrial site protected by best-practice industrial security. They write custom RAT malware to evade antivirus systems and target support technicians at the industrial site using social media research and targeted phishing emails. The support technicians activate malware attachments and authorize administrative privileges for the malware because they believe the malware is a video codec or some other legitimate-seeming technology.

Rather than activate the RAT at the industrial site, where the site's sophisticated intrusion detection systems might detect its operation, the attackers wait until the technician victim is on their home network but needs to log into the industrial site remotely to deal with some problem. The technician activates their VPN and logs in using two-factor authentication. At this point the malware activates, moving the Remote Desktop window to an invisible extension of the laptop's screen and shows the technician a deceptive error message, such as "Remote Desktop has stopped responding. Click here to try to correct the problem."

The malware provides remote control of the invisible Remote Desktop window to the attackers. The technician starts another Remote Desktop session to the industrial site, thinking nothing of the interruption. In this way, sophisticated attackers have access to industrial operations for as long as the technician's laptop and VPN are enabled. The only hint of the problem that the ICS IDS sees is that the technician logged in twice. The attackers eventually learn enough about the system to misoperate the physical process and cause serious damage to equipment or cause an environmental disaster through a discharge of toxic materials.

***Sophistication:*** Currently this requires a high level of cyber sophistication, since no such two-factor-defeating remote-access toolkit is available for free download on the open Internet. To bring about a serious physical consequence within a limited number of remote-access sessions, a high degree of engineering sophistication is required as well.

***Consequence:*** Any attacker willing to invest in the sophisticated, custom malware required for this type of attack will most likely persist in the attack until significant adverse outcomes are achieved.

## #12 IIoT Pivot

Hacktivists unhappy with the environmental practices of an industrial site learn from the popular press that the site is starting to use new, state-of-the-art, Industrial Internet of Things edge devices from a given vendor. The attackers search the media to find other users of the same components, at smaller and presumably less-well-defended sites. The hacktivists target these smaller sites with phishing email and gain a foothold on the IT and ICS networks of the most poorly-defended of these IIoT client sites.

The hacktivists gain access to IIoT equipment at these poorly-defended sites and discover that the equipment is running an older version of Linux with many known vulnerabilities, because the poorly-defended site has not updated the equipment firmware in some time. The attackers take over one of the IIoT devices. After looking at the software installed on the device, they conclude that the device is communicating through the Internet with a database in the cloud from a well-known database vendor. The attackers download Metasploit to the IIoT device and attack the connection to the cloud database with the most recently-released exploits for that database vendor.

They discover that the cloud vendor has not yet applied one of the security updates for the database and the attackers take over the database servers in the cloud vendor. In their study of the relational database and the software on the compromised edge devices, the hacktivists learn that the database has the means to order edge devices to execute arbitrary commands. This is a "support feature" that allows the central cloud site to update software, reconfigure the device, and otherwise manage complexity in the rapidly-evolving code base for the cloud vendor's IIoT edge devices.

The hacktivists use this facility to send commands, standard attack tools and other software to the Linux operating system in the edge devices in the ICS networks the hacktivists regard as their legitimate, environmentally-irresponsible targets. Inside those networks, the attackers use these tools and remote-command facilities to carry out reconnaissance for a time and eventually erase hard drives or cause what other damage they can, triggering unplanned shutdowns.

In short, hacktivists attacked a heavily-defended client of cloud services by pivoting from a poorly-defended client, through a poorly-defended cloud.

*Sophistication:* These attackers are of moderate cyber sophistication. They can download and use public attack tools that can exploit known vulnerabilities, they can launch social engineering and phishing attacks, and they can exploit permissions with stolen credentials. Hacktivists such as these generally have a very limited degree of engineering sophistication.

*Consequences:* Unplanned shutdowns, lost production, and possible equipment damage.

## #13 Malicious Outsourcing

An industrial site has outsourced a remote support function to a control system component vendor – for example: maintenance of the plant historian. The vendor has located their world-wide remote support center in a country with an adequate supply of adequately-educated personnel and low labour costs. A poorly-paid technician at this support center finds a higher-paying job elsewhere. On the last day of employment, this technician decides to take revenge on personnel at a specific industrial client – the same personnel who recently complained to the technician's manager about the technician's performance.

The technician logs into the client site using legitimately-acquired remote access credentials, two-factor credentials and the permanent VPN connection to the targeted site. The technician logs into all the site's control system computers for which the credentials provide access and leaves a small script running on each that, one week later, erases the hard drives on each computer.

*Sophistication:* This is an adversary with limited cyber sophistication and engineering sophistication, who is unable to produce custom malware. This attacker does have credentials and the ability to log into their target remotely and has some knowledge of how that system works – in particular, how to leave a small, simple script running, or schedule such a script to run in the future with administrative privileges.

*Consequences:* The consequences of such an attack vary. For example, no power plant relies on the veracity of its historians for second-by-second operation – at such a target, if the historians were targeted, the consequences would be the loss of historical data since the last backup. Historians targeted at a pharmaceutical plant would more likely trigger the loss of the current batch, since many such plants store their batch records in the historians and are unable to sell products produced in batches whose records are impaired. Such batches can range in value from hundreds of thousands of dollars to hundreds of millions of dollars.

## #14 Compromised Vendor Website

Most sites trust their ICS vendors – but should those vendors' websites be trusted? Hacktivists find a poorly-defended ICS vendor website and compromise it. They download the latest copies of the vendor software and study it. They learn where in the system the name or some other identifier for the industrial site is stored. These attackers are unhappy with a number of industrial enterprises for imagined environmental or other offences and search the public media to determine which of these enterprises use the compromised vendor's software.

The attackers use the compromised website to unpack the latest security update for the ICS software and insert a small script. The attackers repack the security update, sign the modified update with the private key on the web server, and post the hacked update as well as a new MD5 hash for the update.

Over time, many sites download and install the compromised update. At each target, the script activates. If the script fails to find the name of the targeted enterprise in the control system being updated, the script does nothing. When the script finds the name, it installs another small script to active one week later, erasing the hard drive and triggering an unplanned and possibly uncontrolled shutdown. The one-week delay in consequences makes tracing the attack back to the software update somewhat more difficult.

*Sophistication:* This is a hacktivist-class attack, by attackers of moderate cyber sophistication and limited engineering sophistication. The attackers knew enough about computer systems to use existing tools, permissions and vulnerabilities. They also had enough knowledge to unpack control system products and understand to some degree how they work, as well as unpack and repack security updates.

*Consequences:* The most common consequence of this class of attack is an unplanned shutdown. More serious consequences include the potential for equipment damage due to an uncontrolled shutdown.

## #15 Compromised Remote Site

In a SCADA system such as might control an electric distribution system or water distribution system, an attacker targets a substation or pumping station that is physically remote from any potential witnesses. The attacker physically cuts the padlock on a wire fence around the remote station and enters the physical site. The attacker locates the control equipment shed – typically the only roofed building at the site – and again forces the door to gain entry to the shed. The attacker finds the only rack in the small site, plugs a laptop into the Ethernet switch in the rack, and tapes the laptop to the bottom of a piece of computer equipment low in the rack where it is unlikely to be detected. The attacker leaves the site.

An investigation ensues, but the investigators find only physical damage and nothing apparently missing. The extra laptop low in the rack is not noticed. A month later, the attacker parks a car near the remote site and interacts with the laptop via Wi-Fi, enumerating the network and discovering the connections back into the central SCADA site. The attacker uses the laptop to break into equipment at the remote site, and from there into the central SCADA system. The attacker then uses Ukraine-style techniques to cause physical shutdowns.

*Sophistication:* This attack requires physical access to at least one of the remote sites and an investment of physical risk, as well as of equipment in the form of the attack laptop. Hacktivist-class cyber expertise is needed to carry out reconnaissance at the remote site and propagate the attack to the central site. Very limited engineering expertise is needed to bring about a Ukraine-style consequence.

***Consequences:*** Interruptions to the movement of electricity, natural gas, water, or whatever else the SCADA system manages are the simplest consequence of this class of attack. Erased hard drives are another simple consequence. Attackers with a higher degree of engineering sophistication could reprogram protective relays or other equipment protection gear, damaging physical equipment such as transformers and pumps. More sophisticated manipulation of pipeline equipment, especially in pipelines transporting liquids, can result in pressure waves able to cause pipeline breaches and serious leaks.

## #16 Vendor Back Door

A software developer at a software vendor inserts a back door into software used on industrial control systems networks. The software may be ICS software or may be driver, management, operating system, networking, or other software used by ICS components. The back door may have been installed with the approval of the software vendor as a "support mechanism" or may have been installed surreptitiously by a software developer with malicious intent.

The software checks the vendor website weekly for software updates and notifies the user through a message on the screen when an update is available. The software also, unknown to the end user, creates a persistent connection to the update notification website when the website so instructs, and permits personnel with access to the website to operate the machine on the ICS network remotely. Hacktivist-class attackers discover this back door and compromise the vendor's software-update website with a password-phishing attack. The attackers then use the back door to impair operations at industrial sites associated with businesses the hacktivists have imagined that they have some complaint against.

Note that antivirus systems are unlikely to discover this back door, since this is not the autonomously-propagating kind of malware that AV systems are designed to discover. Sandboxing systems are unlikely to discover it either, since the only network-aware behavior observable by those systems is a periodic call to a legitimate vendor's software update site asking for update instructions.

***Sophistication:*** To write the back door into the vendor's product source code and into the update web site's source code requires an intermediate degree of cyber sophistication. Such changes are well within the abilities of the software developers working for the vendor though, since such developers are typically hired to produce code that is much more complex than that needed for this type of back door. A moderate degree of cyber sophistication is required of the hacktivists who discovered the back door.

115

Only limited engineering sophistication is needed to bring about a plant shutdown. Greater sophistication is needed to cause any more than accidental equipment damage.

*Consequences:* Plant shutdowns and erased hard drives are straightforward consequences for hacktivist-class attackers who have carried out this type of attack. More engineering-sophisticated attackers can cause equipment damage and sometimes put worker safety or public safety at risk.

## #17 Stuxnet

Sophisticated attackers target a specific and heavily-defended industrial site. They first compromise a somewhat less-well-defended services supplier, exfiltrating details of how the heavily-protected site is designed and protected. The adversaries develop custom, autonomous malware to target the heavily-defended site specifically and bring about physical damage to equipment at the site. The autonomous malware exploits zero-day vulnerabilities. Service providers carry the malware to the site on removable media. Antivirus scanners are blind to the custom, zero-day-exploiting malware.

*Sophistication:* This class of attack demands a high degree of engineering sophistication to understand the physical process and control system components and to bypass equipment protection and safety systems in an attack. The attack demands a high degree of cyber sophistication as well, to create autonomous, custom malware that is undetectable by the specific cybersecurity technologies deployed at the target site.

*Consequences:* The Natanz uranium enrichment site targeted by Stuxnet is thought to have suffered several months of reduced or zero production of enriched uranium, because of the interference of the Stuxnet worm in the production process. The site is also estimated to have suffered the premature aging and destruction of 1000-2000 uranium gas centrifuge units. More generally, this class of attack can bypass all but physical safety and protection mechanisms and could bring about loss of life, public safety risks and costly equipment damage.

## #18 Hardware Supply Chain

A sophisticated attacker compromises the IT network of an enterprise with a heavily-defended industrial site. The attacker steals information about which vendors supply the industrial site with servers and workstations, as well as which vendors routinely ship such equipment to the site. The attacker then develops a relationship with the delivery drivers in the logistics organization, routinely paying drivers modest sums of money to take two-hour lunch breaks, instead of one-hour breaks.

When IT intelligence indicates that a new shipment of computers is on its way to the industrial site, the agency uses the two-hour window to break into the delivery van, open the packages destined to the industrial site, insert wirelessly-accessible single-board computers into the new equipment, and repackage the new equipment so that the tampering is undetectable. Some time after IT records show that the equipment is in production, the attackers access their embedded computers wirelessly, to manipulate the physical process. The attackers eventually impair equipment protection measures, crippling production at the plant through what appear to be a long sequence of very unfortunate random equipment failures.

*Sophistication:* This is an attack by a very sophisticated adversary. This attacker has physical operatives able to carry out covert actions, such as breaking into the delivery van and quickly disassembling, modifying, reassembling, and repackaging the compromised equipment. The attacker is cyber-sophisticated, maintaining a long-term presence on the target's IT network and understanding the design of a variety of computer equipment well enough to know how to subtly insert additional hardware into that equipment. The attacker has a high degree of engineering sophistication as well, to understand the structure of the physical process, the control systems, and the equipment protection systems in enough detail to design and carry out physical sabotage, making damaged production equipment look like random failures.

*Consequences:* Costly equipment failures and plant production far below targets.

## #19 Nation-State Crypto Compromise

A nation-state grade attacker compromises the PKI encryption system, either by stealing certificates from a well-known certificate authority, or by breaking a popular crypto-system and so forging certificates. The attacker compromises Internet infrastructure to intercept connections from a targeted industrial site to software vendors. The attacker deceives the site into downloading malware with what appears to be a legitimate vendor signature. The malware establishes peer-to-peer communications that are steganographically tunnelled through ICS firewalls and DMZs on what appear to be legitimate vendor-sanctioned communications channels. The nation-state adversary operates the malware by remote control, learning about the targeted site. The adversary creates custom attack tools which, when activated, cause the release of toxins into the environment, serious equipment damage and a plant shutdown.

*Sophistication:* This is a very sophisticated adversary able to defeat the encryption, certificates and cryptographic hashes that are the foundation of IT-SEC security programs.

*Consequences:* Public safety risks and possible loss of life, costly equipment damage and lost production.

## #20 Sophisticated Credentialed ICS Insider

A sophisticated attacker bribes or blackmails an ICS insider at an industrial site. The insider systematically leaks information to the attackers about the design of the site's physical process, control systems and security configurations. The attacker develops custom, autonomous malware designed to defeat the deployed security configurations. The insider deliberately releases the malware on the system with the insider's credentials. A few hours later the malware activates. A day later, there is an explosion that kills several workers, causes a billion dollars in damage to the plant, and shuts the site down for 12-18 months.

*Sophistication:* This is an attacker with a high degree of sophistication in physical operations, able to bribe or blackmail the insider. This attacker has a high degree of engineering sophistication as well, to determine what cyber attack has not been anticipated by the site's safety and equipment protection systems and to determine how to defeat those protections. The attacker also has a high degree of cyber sophistication to produce undetectable, custom, autonomous malware.

*Consequences:* Loss of life, costly equipment damage and lost production.

## Summary

The list of 20 attacks with unacceptable consequences, in rough order of sophistication is summarized in the table below.

| #1 ICS Insider | #6 Ukrainian Attack | #11 Hijacked Two-Factor | #16 Vendor Back Door |
|---|---|---|---|
| #2 IT Insider | #7 Sophisticated Ukrainian Attack | #12 IIoT Pivot | #17 Stuxnet |
| #3 Common Ransomware | #8 Market Manipulation | #13 Malicious Outsourcing | #18 Hardware Supply Chain |
| #4 Targeted Ransomware | #9 Sophisticated Market Manipulation | #14 Compromised Vendor Website | #19 Nation-State Crypto Compromise |
| #5 Zero-Day Ransomware | #10 Cell-phone Wi-Fi | #15 Compromised Remote Site | #20 Sophisticated Credentialed Insider |

With the addition of a Design Basis Threat "line" separating reliably-defeated attacks from those not so defeated, this set of attacks can be used to visualize the difference between different security postures. In the figure below the attacks above the DBT line are not reliably defeated, while those below the line are so defeated.

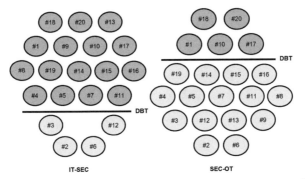

*Figure (30) Illustrating Changes in Security Postures[9]*

This standard list of attacks can also be used to both compare security postures across different sites within an enterprise and compare sites between enterprises and industries.

---

9    This diagram represents IT-SEC and SEC-OT security postures for an example worked in Chapter 12.

# Chapter 12  Assessing Security Programs

This chapter describes the application of the 20 standard attacks to a drinking water treatment plant. Three designs are assessed: an initial IT-SEC design, an IIoT adaptation of the IT-SEC design, and an IIoT SEC-OT design.

## An IT-SEC Water Plant

Consider a water and wastewater treatment system. Cybersecurity priorities for the site include:

1. Worker safety – prevent casualties at the site – safety hazards include large reservoirs and pipes able to fill with water, whether or not site personnel are physically at risk inside those pipes and reservoirs, as well as large reservoirs of toxic chlorine gas and fluoride solutions.

2. Public safety – do not route unclean water or water injected with toxic amounts of fluoride into the water distribution system in quantities that put public safety at risk or that trigger "boil water" advisories.

3. Reliability – manage reservoirs, pumping and treatment systems such that quantities, costs and schedules for clean drinking water comply with service-level agreements with the water distribution utility.

The control system for the plant is protected to IT-SEC-based first-generation ICS security best practices, from circa 2003-2013:

- Only firewalls separate networks at very different levels of criticality.

- Encryption is enabled on all IT and ICS equipment and connections that support such configuration.

- Individual user accounts and passwords are configured on all equipment that supports them, with only the usual exceptions in the ICS space, such as for equipment with only a single account, or HMI workstations that cannot afford to lose visibility into the physical process if operators were to log out and log back in during a shift change.

- The pumping station SCADA WAN uses private, leased telecommunications infrastructure.

- A DMZ separates ICS from IT networks and contains a remote-access jump host, a plant historian, and the plant's Active Directory, AV and other servers synchronized to their respective IT counterparts.

- A comprehensive security-update program is in place. Industrial plant systems cannot be updated as quickly as can IT systems, and because comprehensive testing of the updates on a reliability test-bed takes a long time, most control system components are not updated automatically.

- Antivirus systems are deployed on all equipment that support the corporate AV vendor, with automatic updates.

- Network monitoring information is sent directly from network equipment in the ICS network, through the DMZ, into a central corporate IT NOC/helpdesk in another city.

- Copies of ICS network traffic are fed into a large network intrusion detection analysis engine on the IT network via SPAN and mirror ports on ICS switches.

- Logs, AV alerts, IDS alerts, and other types of security information are sent from ICS equipment to an IT-based SOC.

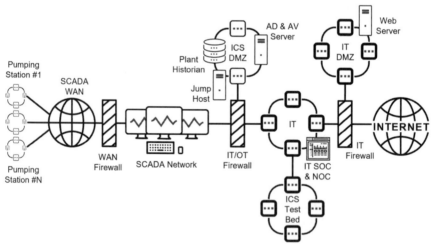

*Figure (31) IT-SEC Water Treatment Plant Network*

Third-party service providers have remote access credentials, can log into IT networks and from IT networks into ICS networks via an ICS DMZ jump host. Policies, procedures, responsibilities and training have been documented and executed according to the IT-SEC best practices of the day.

## Attack Evaluation

Evaluating the 20 example attacks against the above system yields the results below. In the list below, a "defeated" status means the attack is defeated reliably, while "not defeated" means that there is not a high degree of confidence in reliably defeating the indicated attack.

*#1 ICS Insider – not defeated:* None of the indicated security controls prevent an insider from issuing an inappropriate "shut down" command that the insider is authorized to issue.

*#2 IT Insider – defeated:* IT best practices include two-factor authentication for the remote-access jump host, which reliably defeats social-engineered remote access passwords.

*#3 Common Ransomware – defeated:* IT best practices applied to ICS networks mean that ICS equipment cannot browse the Internet or download ransomware. Such best practices also forbid hosts that are configured to execute "AUTORUN" files.

*#4 Targeted Ransomware – not defeated:* Two-factor authentication might prevent the attacker from pivoting through the IT network into the ICS network. A targeted remote-control attack of moderate sophistication, however, can create new accounts on a compromised IT domain controller and two-factor-less accounts on the jump host. Intrusion detection systems on the IT network might or might not detect the attacker, depending on how much effort the attacker is making to minimize their footprint and on how busy the outsourced SOC and enterprise incident response teams are with other apparently higher-priority emergencies.

*#5 Zero-Day Ransomware – not defeated:* The site has a file sharing server set up in the DMZ to minimize the use of USB drives on ICS equipment. Many ICS and IT workstations have access to that server. If the zero-day attack reaches the ICS before antivirus signatures have been updated and before firewall sandbox security updates are in place, the site will be compromised.

*#6 Ukrainian Attack – defeated:* A hacktivist-class attack relies on stolen passwords and known vulnerabilities in network-exposed services. Two-factor authentication defeats stolen passwords and no vulnerabilities are exposed to network attacks.

*#7 Sophisticated Ukrainian Attack – not defeated:* IT-SEC protections do not defeat targeted, low-volume RAT malware reliably. Once inside the network, the described standard remote-control attack techniques are likely to yield the credentials needed to propagate the attack into the ICS network.

Intrusion detection systems on the IT network might detect the attack, depending on how much effort the attackers are making to minimize their footprint and on how busy the outsourced SOC and enterprise incident response teams are with other emergencies.

*#8 Market Manipulation – not defeated:* Drinking water is not a commodity traded on most futures exchanges and so technically this attack does not apply. However, in the interests of illustrating how this attack fares against the indicated protections, this chapter assumes the water site is a legitimate target for market manipulation attacks.

In this case, even when security updates are installed promptly on Internet-facing servers, there may be times when proof-of-concept exploits circulate in the wild for vulnerabilities for which no updates exist yet. Intrusion detection systems may eventually detect the operation of professional attackers using low-grade attack tools, but by then the damage may already be done.

*#9 Sophisticated Market Manipulation – not defeated:* Attackers this sophisticated do not need to log into ICS sites through a jump host – they more often compromise the IT domain controller. Once compromised, the attackers can schedule commands to run on ICS equipment, reaching into DMZ file servers and downloading their low-volume, peer-to-peer, steganographically-encrypted malware. Intrusion detection systems might or might not detect this type of attacker, depending on how much effort the attacker is making to minimize their footprint and on how busy the outsourced SOC and enterprise incident response teams are with other emergencies.

*#10 Cell-phone Wi-Fi – not defeated:* IT best practices do not forbid encrypted Wi-Fi zones in ICS networks. IT best practices do not guarantee that permissions on ICS networks prevent logging into equipment with stolen passwords and erasing hard drives. Intrusion detection systems might report unusual Wi-Fi connections to ICS Wi-Fi networks, but identifying the source of such connections can be difficult and time-consuming. Not all attacks of this class will be reliably detected and remediated in time to prevent consequences.

*#11 Hijacked Two-Factor – not defeated:* This sophisticated attack uses low-volume malware and exploits permissions rather than vulnerabilities, so standard security update and antivirus protections on the technician's laptop are blind to the attack. To intrusion detection systems at the water treatment site, the incoming connection is simply a technician logging into

the control system through the jump host and legitimately manipulating the operation of the control system. All this is normal activity.

*#12 IIoT Pivot – defeated:* There are no IIoT edge devices in the control system and so IIoT-targeted attacks cause no harm.

*#13 Malicious Outsourcing – not defeated:* At least some vendors have remote access through the jump host. Disgruntled employees at these vendors have the opportunity to log into the ICS and impair operations. The consequences of such attacks depend on the cyber and engineering sophistication of the disgruntled attackers.

*#14 Compromised Vendor Website – not defeated:* Antivirus sandbox techniques can have difficulty detecting this class of malware, when the malware activates only on specific machines. Software upgrade testing techniques generally do not include a step where the clock is set forward repeatedly to trigger suspicious behaviour from embedded malware.

*#15 Compromised Remote Site – not defeated:* IT-SEC protections might or might not defeat a hacktivist-class intrusion of this type. The remote site's firewall might be configured to permit connections to a wide range of ICS hosts, providing the hacktivist with a large selection of attack targets, some of which are likely to provide access deeper into the control system. Intrusion detection systems at the central site might, or might not, detect the activity of the hacktivist in time to prevent consequences.

*#16 Vendor Back Door – not defeated:* In ICS networks configured to IT-SEC standards, connections between ICS equipment and specific Internet-based IP addresses belonging to software vendors are often permitted, bypassing the DMZ, precisely to check for security updates. ICS software is generally configured never to update automatically, but a configuration that allows the software to alert site personnel when updates are available is not unusual.

*#17 Stuxnet – not defeated:* Custom malware designed specifically with zero-day exploits to defeat the water utility's security-update, antivirus and intrusion detection systems will defeat those systems.

*#18 Hardware Supply Chain – not defeated:* Depending on the sophistication of the attacker, physical tampering can be made arbitrarily difficult to detect. Intrusion detection systems designed to detect rogue access points may not detect rogue Wi-Fi clients. Host-based protections on existing hosts cannot prevent this kind of supply chain attack from introducing new cyber assets and Wi-Fi communications into a network environment.

*#19 Nation-State Crypto Compromise – not defeated:* Cryptosystems are the foundation of many software-based security technologies. When a cryptosystem is compromised, these protections fail to detect command insertion, falsified security updates and other forgeries.

*#20 Sophisticated Credentialed ICS Insider – not defeated:* It is very difficult to reliably defeat compromised insiders assisting very sophisticated attackers.

Given the analysis above, the DBT for this set of attacks and this target is illustrated:

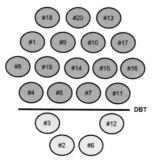

*Figure (32) IT-SEC Design Basis Threat*

In the figure, the attacks below the DBT line are reliably defeated by the IT-SEC/ICS security posture. Those above the line are not defeated reliably.

## Industrial Internet of Things Design

These assessment results can now be used as a baseline to understand the impact of proposed control system and security posture changes. For example, the water site might be considering an upgrade of their control system to use new "Industrial Internet of Things" capabilities:

- Industrial Internet of Things (IIoT) edge devices are sensors and actuators with their own CPUs and software, that do not rely on conventional PLCs or HMIs to operate. IIoT edge devices generally connect directly to Internet-based cloud services with those connections forwarded through multiple layers of ICS firewalls. The cloud services are generally able to receive data from the devices, update firmware in the devices and are often able to send control, optimization and other information to the devices.

- Outsourced "cloud" service providers offer so-called "big data analysis" services as well as other expert-level services to industrial sites. Again, the expectation is that these Internet-based cloud providers have continuous monitoring access to the ICS equipment and software they are monitoring, as well as continuous or on-demand remote access to those systems in order to adjust the systems for optimal performance.

In this example, the water site wishes to deploy vibration, oil quality and other measurement edge devices for all large water pumps and other rotating equipment in the central water treatment site. This means deploying many edge devices from many vendors, with each edge device connected through layers of firewalls to its respective vendor's cloud site or sites. In addition, the site wishes to:

- Outsource security monitoring services to an Internet-based SOC provider,

- Outsource management and support of their primary water treatment ICS software to the software's vendor, and

- Outsource the support and management of several other software applications as well.

The changed elements of the ICS network architecture are illustrated below:

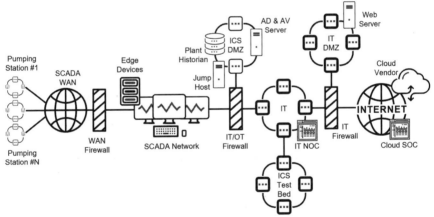

*Figure (33) IIoT Water Treatment Plant Network*

## IIoT Attack Evaluation

The capabilities-based assessment using the top 20 attacks is repeated on the proposed IIoT design for the water treatment system. The results of only two attacks change:

**#3 Common Ransomware – not defeated:** Each new IIoT edge device needs connections to one or more Internet/cloud services. Best practice in non-IIoT installations is to configure IT/OT and other firewalls to permit connections to specific Internet IP addresses only. Since cloud services migrate across the Internet, such rules are impractical for IIoT sites. The water treatment plant, like most IIoT sites, therefore proposed to delete the "deny all access to the Internet" rule from their IT/OT firewall. With the proposed change, equipment on ICS networks can now reach out to Internet sites and download common ransomware.

*#12 IIoT Pivot – not defeated:* Unlike conventional ICS equipment, IIoT edge devices communicate directly with cloud servers rather than moderate their communications through a chain of intervening DMZ networks, servers and protocol changes. This permits attacks to pivot through vendor (cloud) Internet sites much more easily than is the case with conventional ICS components.

The DBT diagram for the proposed changes is contrasted with the original DBT diagram in Figure (34).

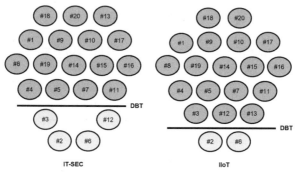

*Figure (34) IT-SEC and IIoT Design Basis Threat*

Most practitioners know instinctively that increased connectivity yields increased attack opportunities and so expect the IIoT security posture to be worse than the original IT-SEC posture. The DBT approach with a standard set of top 20 attacks confirms this instinct and makes the difference easily visible to nontechnical decision makers.

The water utility's business decision makers, seeing this illustration, express dissatisfaction with both the proposed and current states of security in the water treatment utility. When asked to explain these attacks that are not defeated reliably, the security team does so. Explanations of attacks generally start with the simplest attacks that are not defeated reliably, since attackers with a range of attack techniques available to them often choose the simplest, cheapest attacks that work.

No security posture is infallible – there are always attacks above the DBT line. Any site with no such attacks for their security posture either needs to define more powerful attacks or needs to consider whether the effectiveness of their security posture has been misrepresented.

Again, the business decision makers in this example express dissatisfaction, and ask the security team what can be done to improve ICS security, on a limited budget. The team then evaluates a SEC-OT design.

## SEC-OT for The Water System

The security team proposes to implement several SEC-OT practices: unidirectional gateways to protect online communications, strict offline removable media controls and the addition of security testing capabilities to the ICS test bed.

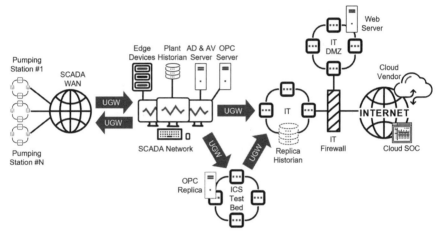

*Figure (35) SEC-OT Water Treatment Plant Network*

The new design defines two control-critical networks at the water treatment site: the main ICS and the test bed. In this initial deployment, pumping stations and the pumping station SCADA WAN are modelled as noncritical ICS networks. The new design uses the following reference architectures:

- **SCADA WAN:** Two independent unidirectional gateways are deployed at the interface to the SCADA WAN, one replicating the SCADA system to pumping stations and one replicating pumping station devices to the SCADA system. In this initial proposal, there are no unidirectional protections deployed in each pumping station. An engineering workstation in a badge-in room at the SCADA site is electrically connected to the private network that implements the SCADA WAN. This workstation provides conventional, encrypted remote access to the pumping stations.

129

- **Database Replication:** A unidirectional gateway is deployed to replicate the plant historian to an IT replica, so that IT applications such as the web server have access to live industrial data.

- **Device Emulation:** A unidirectional gateway replicates the SCADA OPC server to the reliability/security test bed so that the test bed has access to live data for testing.

- **Central or Cloud SOC:** Both the test bed and ICS unidirectional gateways replicate Syslog, SNMP traps, antivirus alerts and other security monitoring information from the test bed to the IT network and through the IT network to the corporate/cloud SOC.

- **Network Intrusion Detection Systems:** The IT/OT and test-bed unidirectional gateways also replicate mirror ports on their respective switches to a network IDS sensor (not illustrated) on the IT network.

## SEC-OT Attack Evaluation

The proposed SEC-OT design is evaluated against the 20 attacks as follows.

*#1 ICS Insider – not defeated:* None of the indicated security controls prevent an insider from issuing an inappropriate "shut down" command that the insider is authorized to issue.

*#2 IT Insider – defeated:* No online message or signal from the IT network has any way to reach the control-critical network. The unidirectional gateways at the IT/OT interface are physically able to send information in only one direction – to the IT network, not from the IT network to the critical network.

*#3 Common Ransomware – defeated:* No browsing of the Internet is possible through a unidirectional gateway. Strict SEC-OT removable media controls mean that no media-resident malware can reach control-critical equipment either.

*#4 Targeted Ransomware – defeated:* No remote-control signal from the IT network or the Internet can reach any control-critical network through the unidirectional gateway.

*#5 Zero-Day Ransomware – defeated:* No ransomware can defeat the unidirectional gateway's physical protection, even with zero-day exploits. Sophisticated, AV-evading ransomware arriving on physical media is deployed first to the isolated test-bed, where the activity of the ransomware is detected by the high-sensitivity IDS either when installed or when the clock on the entire test-bed is advanced to test for time-bombed malware.

*#6 Ukrainian Attack – defeated:* No remote-access or remote-control signal can penetrate the IT/OT gateway, not even with stolen passwords or stolen two-factor authentications.

*#7 Sophisticated Ukrainian Attack – defeated:* No remote-access or remote-control signal can penetrate the IT/OT gateway.

*#8 Market Manipulation – defeated:* No Internet-based attack can reach the unidirectionally-protected critical network.

*#9 Sophisticated Market Manipulation – defeated:* No Internet-based attack can reach the unidirectionally-protected critical network.

*#10 Cell-phone Wi-Fi – not defeated:* In this first-phase SEC-OT plan, the security team did not propose forbidding encrypted Wi-Fi zones in control-critical networks, nor did the site forbid cell phones. Scanning for such networks, phishing passwords and connecting to the networks via compromised cell phones is still possible.

*#11 Hijacked Two-Factor – defeated:* No Internet-based attack can reach the unidirectionally-protected critical network. Remote support, when needed, can be carried out with unidirectional Remote Screen View, which makes screens from workstations on control-critical networks visible to web browsers on external IT and Internet networks. Such visibility though, confers no ability for the remote user to control the critical workstations. Control must be carried out by insiders with access to the indicated workstations' mice and keyboards, usually with a voice connection to external support personnel who provide verbal advice to site personnel, based on the contents of the live screen images replicated to the support provider.

*#12 IIoT Pivot – defeated:* No Internet-based attack can reach the unidirectionally-protected critical network.

*#13 Malicious Outsourcing – defeated:* No attack from any external vendor network can reach the unidirectionally-protected networks. Again, any vendor access to a critical network is via Remote Screen View. Engineers at the site will schedule the execution of software into the future on multiple machines only when they have a clear understanding of the reason for, and consequences of, such execution.

*#14 Compromised Vendor Website – defeated:* All new vendor software is deployed first on the reliability/security test bed. In this attack scenario, the software detects that it has been installed on what appears to be a fully-functional industrial network. When the clock on the test bed is advanced,

131

the malware activates, erasing hard drives. The test bed is quickly restored from backup images, with no harm done to the critical network.

**#15 Compromised Remote Site – defeated:** The unidirectional gateway replicating SCADA system instructions to remote sites across the SCADA WAN is not physically able to transmit any attack information back into the control-critical network. The gateway oriented to monitor remote sites is unable to open new connections from a compromised remote site into the critical network – the gateway is a client of devices at remote sites, not a server that forwards arbitrary attack files, or a firewall or router that forwards arbitrary attack packets.

**#16 Vendor Back Door – defeated:** Unidirectional gateways are not routers, are unidirectional, and for both reasons are unable to propagate TCP connections from malware on control-critical devices to command and control centers, whether or not those control centers are part of ICS-vendor websites.

**#17 Stuxnet – not defeated:** The consequences of malware such as the historical Stuxnet worm may not be visible on test-bed networks, however faithfully those test beds try to emulate an ICS environment. The consequences of Stuxnet were visible only in the physical process.

**#18 Hardware Supply Chain – not defeated:** Malicious behaviour of new equipment might be observed by the high-sensitivity IDS on the test-bed network. However, attackers who know this test bed exists might also know how long new equipment is tested on the test-bed before being deployed into production. Attackers could simply delay their use of malicious hardware until they are confident that the hardware has passed test and is deployed on the production SCADA system.

**#19 Nation-State Crypto Compromise – defeated:** Protections for the ICS network are physically unidirectional, not software-based or cryptographic.

**#20 Sophisticated Credentialed ICS Insider – not defeated:** It is very difficult to reliably defeat compromised insiders who are cooperating with sophisticated attackers.

A DBT summary for the analysis above is compared to the summaries from the IT-SEC and IIoT security postures in Figure (36). The SEC-OT security program reliably defeats a much larger set of attacks than does the IT-SEC program. Residual risks in the new DBT are all risks that require physical access to the SCADA site, or very costly and sophisticated attacks from the most sophisticated of nation-state-grade adversaries.

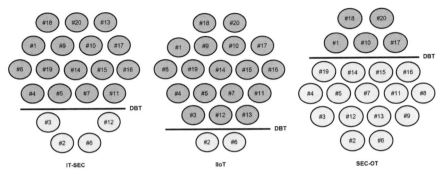

*Figure (36) SEC-OT Design Basis Threat*

In this example, business decision-makers can easily see and understand the improvement in the proposed security posture. This makes it easier for these decision-makers to decide which risks are acceptable and which justify authorization and funding for security program changes.

## Summary

This chapter applies 20 standard cyber attacks to three security postures for a water treatment plant:

1. A design inspired by IT-SEC principles, reflecting ICS security best practice advice from circa 2003-2013,

2. That same design modified to accommodate modern IIoT equipment and practices, and

3. The IIoT design modified to reflect modern SEC-OT principles, though only a subset of SEC-OT principles was applied.

The DBT summary diagram clearly indicates how the IIoT architecture was weaker than the IT-SEC architecture, and how the SEC-OT approach was stronger than either of the competing designs.

# Chapter 13  Advanced Topics

This chapter considers advanced topics and next steps for SEC-OT.

## Physical Safety Equipment

There are voices in some industrial enterprises who argue that physical safety systems and analog equipment protection systems deployed in their industrial process obviate the need for cybersecurity protections. They argue that over-pressure valves, over-speed governors, over-torque clutches and other physical or analog safety systems protect physical operations without software and without the possibility of cyber compromise. Other experts advocate increasing the deployment of such analog, physical safety and equipment-protective systems instead of investing in cybersecurity protections. These opinions have some merit.

> **Note**
>
> *When considering consequences in cyber risk assessments, SEC-OT practitioners should always consult with safety systems engineers regarding safety designs and equipment at the site.*

The possible consequences of cyber attacks are often constrained by physical and analog safety designs at industrial sites. When carrying out risk assessments, any correct assessment of risks and consequences must take such protections and constraints into account.

However, as was the case with air gaps, many well-meaning practitioners at industrial sites have naive impressions that all potential safety and equipment-damaging conditions have been mitigated physically. A detailed inspection of physical equipment, or of as-built physical and analog protections often reveals that either:

- These impressions are mistaken – physical protections are not comprehensive and cyber compromise can still result in unacceptable safety or equipment-damaging consequences,

- Even when comprehensive physical protections are in place, these protections are designed to prevent the consequences of accidental or random equipment failures, not the consequences of simultaneous failures that may be engineered as part of a cyber attack, and/or

- Digital protections were designed into safety and equipment protection programs as an essential layer of defence and redundancy – a cyber

135

attack that disables these defences degrades protections to the point where an immediate safety shutdown is still required.

More to the point for SEC-OT sites though:

> **Note**
>
> *Physical and analog safety and protection equipment, even when that equipment works flawlessly, prevents only safety and equipment-damaging consequences.*
>
> *Analog equipment does not prevent the site shutdowns and impaired production that are the simplest consequences of cyber attacks.*

Most SEC-OT sites regard a site shutdown and impaired production quantity or quality as unacceptable consequences. Physical safety equipment protects safety, not continuous productive operations.

Deploying physical protections for safety and equipment protection wherever practical is a best practice, but generally does not obviate the need for a robust SEC-OT program.

## On-Demand Remote Access

There are voices in many industrial enterprises who argue that IT-SEC, VPN-ed, two-factor, on-demand interactive remote access is essential to industrial operations. They argue, for example, that such access is essential to recruiting young workers who would much rather work in their basements in the suburbs than battle traffic to reach a physically-secured central engineering site every day or drive to a distant industrial site to do their work. These voices argue that since IT-SEC protections are sufficient for IT networks, such protections must also suffice for ICS networks.

SEC-OT forbids designs that permit such remote access to control-critical networks. The only way to provide continuous, on-demand remote access to every Internet-connected computer on the planet is via layers of firewalls, encryption and other software-based compensating measures. Persuading these voices and the business decision-makers who authorize remote access policy is the reason for the introduction to capabilities-based risk assessment included in this book's Chapters 10-12.

Many ICS security practitioners though, are already close to recognizing the dangers of this type of undisciplined remote access, and sometimes need only to be led through a chain of reasoning to change their perceptions. Consider a conversation this author had with two security practitioners at a refinery, one practitioner in charge of IT security and the other ICS security.

One practitioner expressed the concern, "I don't see how we can adopt this approach – it means that we will not be able to access our plants remotely any more."

This author responds, "I see. Tell me – in your existing remote access system, how many machines on the open Internet are authorized to reprogram the PLCs in your refineries?"

The practitioner replies "None! On the Internet? What are you talking about?"

The author adds, "Well – when you are in your hotel room after a day at a conference and you fire up the VPN to connect to the refinery and check how your latest change is working, your laptop is on the Internet isn't it? And you are using it to look at and possibly reprogram the refinery's PLCs."

The practitioner pauses, and responds, "Hmm – I never thought of it that way."

"So, how many machines?" asks the author.

"I'm not sure – I'll have to think about that." is the response.

"Here is an easier question – how many computers on your IT network are authorized to reprogram the PLCs in your refineries?"

"None! No. Wait." A pause. "I'll have to think about that one as well."

At this point the one practitioner turns to the other, who was silent through the exchange, and says: "This is what you've been trying to tell me for the last year isn't it?"

The second nods his head once, slowly. The first says "I get it now." He turns back to the author. "Please continue."

Awareness of the dangers of on-demand, software-only remote access is increasing. When a specific kind of remote access really is vital to operations, SEC-OT advocates deploying the most secure unidirectional reference architecture that meets the requirement, rather than opening up the entire control-critical network to attack by deploying only software-based protections.

## SEC-OT Anti-Patterns

A small number of design errors crop up frequently in teams new to the SEC-OT methodology. Such errors rarely persist long enough to jeopardize deployments but can confuse and delay deployments.

### *Replicating TCP*

Some teams are drawn to the mistaken idea that they can "replicate TCP" unidirectionally. These teams reason that essentially all IP-based industrial communications protocols use TCP, as do the vast majority of IT applications and servers. These teams reason that rather than replicating databases and emulating devices, they can simply "replicate TCP unidirectionally" to reap the benefits of unidirectional gateways.

In fact, almost all TCP-based protocols are poll/response or query/response at the application layer of the protocol. It matters not that some sort of unidirectional TCP emulation can adjust sequence numbers and forge three-way handshakes in the transport layer: the query/response nature of application layer protocols means that those protocols will not work across a unidirectional medium. Database, device and server replication is essential to transparent unidirectional communications.

An industrial site that insists on searching may find a unidirectional technology provider who will sell the site a pair of unidirectional components, one oriented out of the ICS network and one back into it, forwarding TCP packets in both directions. Now the site can forward database and other query packets through one unidirectional connection and forward the answers back through the other.

Such a design is a serious mistake. How much more secure is this than a firewall? Inbound queries can encode attacks. Outbound responses can provide attack feedback to a remote attacker. Capturing arbitrary TCP traffic as files, automatically transmitting those files into a control-critical network and automatically transmitting responses back to IT applications as files is equally poor design. Any design that automatically transmits arbitrary information into ICS networks is of concern. Even more problematic is a design that transmits arbitrary information into ICS networks and transmits arbitrary responses and attack feedback out to IT-network or Internet attackers.

Unidirectional gateways and all SEC-OT unidirectional reference architectures replicate servers and emulate devices for a reason – such replication is the right way to exploit the physical protections of a unidirectional gateway.

### *Replicating Arbitrary Files*

Replicating arbitrarily complex files unidirectionally from critical networks to IT networks permits no information/attack flows to reach control-critical networks. However, setting up a unidirectional gateway to replicate arbitrary files back into a critical network is most often a mistake.

Cyber attacks are often embedded in complex files such as PDF files, ZIP files and word processing documents. Deploying a gateway to forward such files into a critical-network file share almost assures the propagation of malware into the critical network. When common malware compromises an IT asset, the malware frequently copies itself to all file shares to which the IT asset has access, including the share from which files are sent unidirectionally into the critical network. Targeted attacks do the same thing, though less frequently, less noisily and so in a manner that is harder to detect.

When complex files need to be transferred routinely into a control-critical network, the safest such transfers use a software client that actively seeks out, validates and transfers the files, rather than replicating arbitrary files and file servers. For example, a reversible unidirectional gateway configured to send complex antivirus signature updates into a protected network should:

- Fetch the antivirus signature files from an authoritative source, such as the AV vendor's website, or a local AV server, not wait for some person or software to drop the signature file or some other arbitrary file into a file share.

- After fetching what appears to be the correct file, the software should authenticate the file. In the AV case, ensure that the file is signed by a public key controlled by the AV vendor.

- After transferring the file to the protected network, the reversible gateway software should again authenticate the file, in case the software authentication mechanism on the IT-exposed side of the gateway was compromised or somehow impaired.

Only after all of this, should the software forward the file into the protected network for further testing, processing or application.

## First Steps

The end goal for a SEC-OT site is the deployment of thorough physical protections from offline and online information flows/attacks, coupled with additional layers of IT-SEC software compensating measures. The most mature SEC-OT sites modify a small number of IT-SEC compensating measures as indicated in Chapter 9 but deploy essentially all relevant SEC-OT and IT-SEC measures as universally as is practical.

While this end goal is clear, a reasonable set of first steps towards that goal is less obvious. Most sites transitioning to SEC-OT deploy at minimum:

- **Unidirectional network reference architectures:** deploy such architectures sufficient to physically prevent most or all online information/attack flows from entering control-critical networks from external networks. This defeats essentially all online attacks, including common ransomware downloads, targeted ransomware and sophisticated remote-control, nation-state attacks.

- **Removable media protections:** Deploy as much of the removable media program as practical, including physically disabling the mounting of removable media on as much equipment as possible and installing frequently-updated antivirus software on all equipment where the use of removable media is still physically possible. In a "first step" many sites model USB drives as removable media, even though they are more properly modelled as removable devices. "First step" sites generally also train their personnel that files may be copied to removable media destined for critical networks only from IT cyber assets that are completely up to date with the latest security updates and antivirus signatures.

- **Removable device protections:** Deploy as much of the removable device program as practical. At minimum, "first step" sites train their personnel that laptop computers are dangerous. Such sites may still permit vendors to bring laptops to site, but only if the vendors can demonstrate that the laptops are completely up to date with IT-SEC precautions including: being up to date with respect to security updates, having the latest antivirus signatures installed and activated, and showing evidence of a recent complete AV scan of the laptop.

Industrial sites at the very beginning of their industrial security programs are sometimes faced with completely "flat" IP networks, where ICS computers share the same IP address space as IT computers. While this situation can be a serious impediment to IT-SEC firewall deployments, it is less troubling for a transition to SEC-OT.

SEC-OT offline best practices have nothing to do with IP addressing. Unidirectional gateways permit sites to use the same IP address space on both source and destination networks. Renumbering IP addresses in a control system is not a prerequisite for segmenting networks using unidirectional gateways.

## Parting Thoughts

SEC-OT sites set their cyber DBT "bar" very high. One might expect that setting a high standard is costly, but SEC-OT sites report the opposite. Such sites report that the capital cost of an IT-SEC program for ICS networks is comparable to the capital cost of an SEC-OT program, the operating costs for SEC-OT are lower, and SEC-OT security benefits to ICS networks are much higher, as was illustrated in Chapter 12.

The most significant operating cost reductions at SEC-OT sites generally arise from reducing the frequency of costly security updates and reducing the risk of downtime due to inadequately-tested security updates that impair ICS operations. Secondary cost reductions come from reduced security management costs, such as a reduced rate of ICS network intrusion false alarms that must be investigated, reduced costs for managing complex IT/OT and ICS DMZ firewall configurations, and reduced security and compliance documentation costs for the entire SEC-OT-protected network.

The rate of adoption of SEC-OT is increasing. This is no surprise, given that automation of industrial processes continues to increase, attack sophistication continues to increase, and so the risk of unacceptable physical consequences of cyber compromise continue to increase. Regulations, standards and best-practice guidance documents are all increasingly recognizing SEC-OT principles and best practices. New standards and advice produced since about 2014 generally documents how SEC-OT-style physical protections fit into ICS security programs, protections including removable media controls, removable device controls and unidirectional gateway technology.

In short, there are many drivers for the adoption of the principles and practices gathered together in this book and called SEC-OT. The question is not whether ICS networks will see much more widespread adoption of SEC-OT principles, but when.

# Appendix A: Acronyms

| | |
|---|---|
| AV | Antivirus |
| CPU | Central Processing Unit |
| DBT | Design-Basis Threat |
| DCS | Distributed Control System |
| DMZ | Demilitarized Zone |
| ERP | Enterprise Resource Planning |
| HMI | Human-Machine Interface |
| HVAC | Heating, Ventilation and Air Conditioning |
| IDS | Intrusion Detection System |
| IACS | Industrial Automation and Control System |
| ICS | Industrial Control System |
| IIoT | Industrial Internet of Things |
| IP | Internet Protocol |
| IT | Information Technology |
| IT-SEC | Information Technology Security |
| LAN | Local-Area Network |
| MPLS | Multiprotocol Label Switching |
| NAC | Network Access Control |
| NIDS | Network Intrusion Detection System |
| NOC | Network Operations Center |
| NSA | National Security Agency |
| OSHA | Occupational Safety and Health Administration |
| OPC | Not an acronym – part of the name of the OPC Foundation |
| OT | Operations Technology |
| PDF | Portable Document Format |
| PLC | Programmable Logic Controller |
| PMU | Phasor Measurement Units |
| RAT | Remote Access Trojan |
| RBAC | Role-Based Access Control |
| RTU | Remote Terminal Unit |
| SCADA | Supervisory Control and Data Acquisition |
| SEC-OT | Secure Operations Technology |
| SIEM | Security Information and Event Management |
| SIS | Safety-Instrumented System |
| SOC | Security Operations Center |

| | |
|---|---|
| SPAN | Switched Port Analyzer |
| TCP | Transport Control Protocol |
| TPM | Trusted Platform Module |
| UGW | Unidirectional Gateway |
| WAN | Wide-Area Network |

## About the Author

Andrew Ginter lives in Calgary, Alberta, Canada. He holds a BSc. in Applied Mathematics and an MSc. in Computer Science, both from the University of Calgary. He is the author of *SCADA Security – What's broken and how to fix it* and a coauthor of the *Industrial Internet Consortium Security Framework*.

Andrew spent a decade developing control system software products for Hewlett Packard, Agilent Technologies and other vendors. He spent half a decade developing IT/OT middleware products for Agilent Technologies and Verano. These products connected control and manufacturing networks to IT networks, thereby contributing to the industrial security problems that now plague many industries. This last 14 years Andrew spent as CTO and CSO at Industrial Defender and then VP Industrial Security at Waterfall Security Solutions, working to design, develop and deploy industrial security products and technologies. Andrew is also an Adjunct Assistant Professor at Michigan Technological University teaching a graduate course on cyber risk assessment for critical infrastructures.

Andrew is the eldest of seven children born to refugees who made a new life in a strange land and worked hard to live their faith and raise their children. He is married 30 years to a woman he adores, has two grown daughters of whom he is enormously proud, and writes in his spare time.